THE HASKELL MEMOIRS

Colonel John Cheves Haskell in His Confederate Uniform.

The
Haskell Memoirs

JOHN CHEVES HASKELL

Edited by
Gilbert E. Govan and James W. Livingood

G. P. PUTNAM'S SONS   NEW YORK

© *1960 by Gilbert E. Govan and James W. Livingood*

Published on the same day in the Dominion of Canada by Longmans, Green & Company, Toronto.

Library of Congress Catalog
Card Number: 60-8469

MANUFACTURED IN THE UNITED STATES OF AMERICA

VAN REES PRESS • NEW YORK

Author's Preface

I have been so urged by my friends and family to write something of my experiences in the Confederate War that I have, after much hesitation, decided to attempt it and leave its disposition to my family. I have always felt unwilling to publish anything of what I saw during the war because it has been my experience that it is practically impossible for one writing to avoid giving undue prominence to those fragments of the picture in which he took part. Even if he exaggerates nothing and misstates nothing, yet by giving only what he saw or did he apparently excludes acts of more importance and actors who did more.

Having been actively engaged in many of the most active scenes of the war I have never yet seen a record of any part of it which, read by one having no personal knowledge of the facts written of, would fail to give an utterly wrong impression and do grave injustice, by giving seemingly to the writer or to those of whom he writes position and credit to which others were at least partly entitled. It would be without intentional misrepresentation but because the writer saw only one side of the shield and could write only of what he saw. Perhaps it was the silver side, while the gold side got no record, not

v

because the writer would deny it but simply because he did not see it. Nonetheless he will rank in the judgment of those he failed to give credit to as a liar; yet he told only the truth and told all he knew.

I have so often thought that written statements were false and afterwards found they were true, although only part of the truth and so presented as to give almost as false an impression as if wholly false. I have consequently feared that should I undertake to write I might make grave mistakes or tell only some of the facts, leaving out others of more importance; or by telling only those which I knew give them undue weight and thus appear to claim credit to which others are better entitled and of which I do not intend to deprive them.

For these reasons I am, even while writing, full of doubt and hesitation as to the breaking of my long kept resolution. On the other hand, as time passes it becomes more important that the testimony of each witness be recorded for possible use in making up the record. I have decided therefore to write some of what I saw, and leave it to the judgment of my family to decide if it shall be used.

In December 1860 the whole state of South Carolina was in ferment. Many experienced men as well as all the young and inexperienced had gone wild on the subject of secession, and were anxious that Lincoln should be elected. It was believed that his election would sweep the South from the Union over the opposition of those who did not favor secession and were regarded almost as traitors.

I well remember the night when the news came that Lincoln was probably elected. I with a party of other college boys went to Hunt's Hotel [in Columbia], where several speeches were made. Among the speakers was F. J. Moses, a prominent lawyer from Sumter, who in a most violent secession speech hoped the report of the election was true, as it would sweep away the opposition of the weak-kneed and hesitating, like his valued and timid friend, Wade Hampton. Moses lived to be a prominent member of the infamous carpetbag government that wrecked the State from 1868 to 1876. He was Chief Justice of the Court of Appeals, while his son, F. J., Jr., was for years the leader in all the worst thievery and corruption, winding up as Governor.

Neither father nor son ever went into the army. His "timid" friend, Wade Hampton, entered the war and his history is a large part of that in the next four years. His next appearance was when the State called him in '76, when the carpetbaggers and their allies were turned out, the Moses, father and son, being among those deposed at that time. Justice Moses rendered honest decisions, which were of great benefit, and was generally believed to be in sympathy with the decent people of the State. His son was to the last allied with the lowest element of the plunderers, and led a vigorous fight in their own party against D. H. Chamberlain, who refused to sign the commission of the younger Moses as judge, a position which he sought only for the opportunities it would give him to sell decisions.

Chamberlain, who was governor from 1874 through 1876, took the ground boldly that the younger Moses and W. J. Whipper, both of whom had been elected judge, were unfit and that he would not give his assent to their being put on the bench to disgrace it. Chamberlain's course was one of the first steps toward a better state of things, and it was a heavy blow at the Reconstruction party, whose only bond was plunder. It made a most effective break in their party, which cared nothing for success except as it meant free plunder. They considered Chamberlain's efforts to make their party honest and decent a blow at the only liberty they valued, License.

Chamberlain was one of the few men of character and education who came South after the war. Even they believed that Northern thrift and economy would reap rich harvests from the development of the South's great natural resources.

They did not realize the insuperable difficulties of working with labor which for generations had been but irresponsible chattels, whose one idea of freedom was license, whose foresight never looked beyond the needs of the day, and who could not realize that with the power to govern themselves had come the burden of supporting themselves, the helpless children, and old people, who had been cared for as well as controlled.

Some of the Northerners thought they could direct the ignorant, grateful negro, even making rich profits while elevating the former slave. But they either gave up in despair, losing all they had put in, or went with the crowd and made profit of their intelligence in a division of plunder. Those who failed in an effort to make an honest government are still entitled to much credit. They did much to counteract the great wrong they did the South by attempting to control its destiny and giving a kind of moral support to what would, if left to itself, have perished of its own corruption in a tithe of the time that it stood, a blighting pestilence over the whole South.

I have given what I remember of these events, and have written hurriedly and without order. I have tried to give as a narrative part of what I saw and lived through, fully recognizing that I have omitted many things which in justice to others should be recorded. But I could only give the side of the shield I saw, and that most imperfectly, for after the passage of thirty-eight years, writing solely from memory, the most I can hope is not to have misstated anything. I may have done others an injustice by not telling things to their credit. I have not done so intentionally and hope that I have not done so at all.

JOHN C. HASKELL

Foreword

John Cheves Haskell was past sixty years of age when he sat down to write his reminiscences of his service with the Confederate army. Almost four decades had elapsed since the surrender in April 1865 which marked an end of the Confederacy but did not terminate the great emotional experience which Americans of that generation had known. Like many other old soldiers of the time, days in the field and in desperate action dominated his daily conversation; but Colonel Haskell only reluctantly wrote his account so that his family would have his record. His interest was not in publication, but he left that decision to his heirs.

Approximately forty more years had elapsed when Haskell's memoirs came to the attention of the historian Douglas Southall Freeman. Dr. Freeman used them in the writing of *Lee's Lieutenants*. Although he warned in one instance that he found Haskell confused the sequence of events too badly to be followed, he found the text in its entirety to be "charming memoirs." Since Freeman, several other scholars have had an opportunity to see the manuscript and have commented on the vivid quality of the writing and the forthrightness of the opinions expressed. While these values are of fundamental importance to the scholar, they also are characteristics which make a publication of interest to the general reader.

Although in his evaluation of events and individuals Haskell at times called on his knowledge of the total war, his account is largely related to his own firsthand experiences. As a youth of nineteen he quit the quiet of the college campus to take his place in the ranks with fellow South Carolinians before the fateful action at Fort Sumter. He had had no military training or experience, so he had no choice as to the branch of the army he might join; his only interest was to get into service as quickly as possible. Haskell, however, didn't think in terms of "a picnic-war." He was a very serious young man whose views reflected family tradition rooted deeply in Carolina tidewater plantation life. His was a sense of mission, the defense of a cause which allowed no compromise with issue or self. Discipline and duty were moral obligations. Their zealous pursuit produced an optimistic patriotism and a ceaseless demand on the physical and moral fibers of the young soldier. Neither privation nor menial duties drew complaint; nor did bodily wounds or the suffering and death of comrades detract from a determination to serve. Defeat was recognized only with the ultimate failure of the cause.

This individual approach to the war was not unique in young Haskell. Many of his comrades were no less selfish. But it was a remarkably consistent view in the Haskell family. When John assumed the role of volunteer aide in April 1861, four of his brothers were also on duty on the beaches in the Charleston neighborhood. Two younger brothers eventually also volunteered and all served until final surrender with the exception of two who gave their lives for the South.

Few Confederate families contributed more to the cause than the Haskells. Since John in his memoirs concentrated on his own experiences mainly, the editors decided it would be well to bring together in an appendix the fascinating saga of all the members of the family who wore the Southern uniform. Since the assignments of all but one of them were largely in various organizations of the Army of Northern Virginia, their record becomes to a degree a personalized history of that famous army's participation in the war.

John Cheves Haskell became a seasoned campaigner while serving in a number of minor capacities in the first years of the war. Not until the early months of 1863 did he receive assignment to the command of a battery of artillery, that fighting branch in which he had such a distinguished career. In writing of him after the struggle Gordon McCabe called Haskell "a glorious young battalion commander, whose name will be forever associated with the Artillery Corps of the Army of Northern Virginia"; and Jennings Wise in *The Long Arm of Lee*, a history of the artillery that served under Lee, added the adjective "superb" for his estimate of the Colonel. Haskell was a member of a small, select group of young officers who distinguished themselves in this demanding service—Pelham and Pegram were two others—so it was entirely fitting that General Lee chose him to lead the Confederate guns to the place of surrender at Appomattox.

Haskell's behavior in the service from the beginning won the wholehearted praise of his superiors, which is modestly undisclosed in his memoirs. In his account of his experiences at Gaines's Mill where he seemed without fear he writes with typical matter-of-fact directness, yet his conduct here brought commendation from five generals—Longstreet, D. R. Jones, A. P. Hill, Magruder, and Whiting. Even when he had his photograph taken after the loss of his arm, Haskell carefully arranged the empty sleeve so that the viewer gets the impression that the arm was still there. Young as he was, he wanted neither sympathy nor concessions because of his injury.

In his relations with others, Haskell was generous but forthright. If he had an opinion he stated it frankly and without regard for consequences. When in the spring of 1863 he disagreed with the conduct of D. H. Hill in the North Carolina campaign, he did not conceal his attitude but asked to be transferred. He exhibits the same trait in his memoirs where he writes frankly of shortcomings and records his observations and the opinions he had heard of men and events without apology. Those things which he himself saw, he had no fear about; those of which he heard, he measured against a single criterion: did they have the ring of truth? If so, he put them down, even though it might cause resentment among individuals who adulated without reason.

That was consistently a characteristic of the man. The writer of his obituary in *The Columbia State* noted it with emphatic phrase: "He was a man of analytical mind and of uncompromising character. In the days when political revolution swept the State he might have been a popular idol, but he struck true to what he conceived to be principle—and there he was ever found."

After the war, Haskell married Sarah Hampton, daughter of Wade Hampton, and after her death, her cousin Lucy Hampton. He moved to Mississippi and operated a plantation, but in a few years returned to Columbia, South Carolina, where he began the practice of law, a profession in which he earned lifelong distinction. In 1877 he was elected to the state legislature at a time when the Reconstruction government was terminated in a dramatic campaign which placed his father-in-law in the governor's mansion. As recognition for faithful service the electorate returned Haskell to his position until 1890. At his death in Columbia, June 26, 1906, he was survived by his wife and four children: Preston H. Haskell, Frank H. Haskell, Dr. Charles C. Haskell, and Mrs. Frank Lindsay.

During these years there was slight possibility that details of the war experiences were forgotten. The Haskell clan certainly discussed them on many occasions and in the company of a Hampton one cannot imagine a conversation in which reference was not made to days in the field. And there were many hundreds of other veterans living in the Palmetto State. To the knowledge of the editors, there are but few major errors in the memoirs. Although the Colonel wrote from memory without the aid of a war journal and apparently without his letters which he had written home, details were ever fresh in his mind.

Some errors did creep into his writing but they are understandable. Even those noted by Dr. Freeman about the fighting of May 6, 1864, in the Wilderness, where Haskell confused somewhat the sequence of events and said that the conference between Longstreet and Lee was long, not brief, were actually only relative. It is possible that some of the mistakes were not Haskell's but those of his typist or typists. He wrote in longhand and someone copied the manuscript at an unknown time.

Actually the editors have found three copies of the manuscript, no two of them agreeing in their entirety. Sometimes sentences are run together or sections of the narrative are dropped. None of them contains the account of the fighting on October 7, 1864, the action in which he and his brother Aleck were wounded, although Haskell specifically states in one place that he had written about it in a different section of the manuscript. One of the copies lacks entirely the section in Chapter 7 about the Dudleys, the departure of Willis, and the meeting with Lewis Haskell, yet it is in both the other copies. Another has two different beginnings, evidence that at some time after writing one, he became dissatisfied and started again. On the whole, however, all three coincide and at no place does any of them contradict a conclusion or opinion in the others.

This book is a composite of the three manuscripts. In some ways the editors have made changes. Related matters have been brought together where found widely scattered in the manuscript. The more clear or better-expressed passages of the three manuscripts are used where choice was possible.

Punctuation and paragraphing have also been modified as an aid to the reader.

The editors have drawn generously upon Louise Haskell Daly's *Alexander Cheves Haskell: The Portrait of a Man* for family material, and are grateful for the generous assistance they have received from other people and institutions in the preparation of the manuscript for publication. The editors wish to acknowledge their indebtedness to several members of the Haskell family: to the late Mrs. Preston H. Haskell, Sr., who gave the permission to publish the memoirs, and to her son, Preston H. Haskell, Jr.; to Mrs. Marian Haskell Raoul for permission to quote from some of the letters of her father, Alexander C. Haskell.

Our sincere thanks and deep appreciation can only be expressed inadequately to Mr. Gaston C. Raoul for his unflagging interest in the project and for his assistance in securing information from members of the Haskell family, and to Mrs. Alice Haskell Benet, who gave valuable help in securing the obituary of Colonel Haskell. Professional assistance was also generously given by Mrs. Pat Bryant, Georgia Department of Archives and History, Atlanta; Mrs. Louise I. Catterall, The Valentine Museum, Richmond; Dewey E. Carroll, Emory University Library, Atlanta; Miss Theresa D. Hodges, Librarian of the Petersburg Public Library; Dr. J. H. Easterby of the South Carolina Department of Archives, and by the staff of the Columbia Public Library. For financial assistance we are indebted to the Committee for Research and Creative Activity of the University of Chattanooga.

GILBERT E. GOVAN

JAMES W. LIVINGOOD

November 19, 1959

Contents

THE HASKELL MEMOIRS

Chapter 1

To Arms!

IN December, 1860, I was a student in the South Carolina College [1] and went home to Abbeville for the Christmas vacation. My brother William had just left the University of Virginia and my brother Aleck just graduated at the South Carolina College. My father lived at the home place which was eleven miles from Abbeville Court House. The nearest railroad station was there, while Columbia was, until after the war, the nearest telegraph office.

While we were all at dinner, about Christmas day or a day or two before, a messenger who had been sent to Abbeville for the mail came out and brought with him the papers containing the proceedings of the Secession Convention [2] then sitting and a note from Colonel James Perrin [3] of Abbeville, saying he had a letter from Colonel Maxcy Gregg, [4] who had just been appointed a colonel with authority to raise a regiment. Colonel Gregg had written, inviting Colonel Perrin to raise a company for said regiment. My two brothers, William and Aleck, at once announced their intention to join his company, and I began to follow suit, when my father, who was very much accustomed to rule in his own house, stopped me most peremptorily. He said he did not care to hear anything further

3

on the subject and that I should not go till I came of age. I submitted for the time being but went back to college very much dissatisfied, and in April, hearing that Fort Sumter was to be attacked, I left on the next train, only to find when I got to Charleston that martial law had been declared and I could not get to Morris Island,[5] where was posted Gregg's Regiment, which I wished to join.

That evening when the boat for Sullivan's Island [6] was about to start, I went to the hotel clerk to consult him as to the possibility of getting to Morris Island. A tall man in the uniform of the United States Army, overhearing me, asked what I wanted. I answered that I wanted to get to Gregg's Regiment, where I had two brothers whom I wanted to join. He asked my name and on hearing it asked if I were related to Captain Charles Haskell of the First Regulars (a regiment authorized, together with a battalion of artillery, by the convention to form the Regular Army of the Republic of South Carolina, both being then stationed at Sullivan's Island). On my telling him that Charles was my brother, he said that he could take me there, as he was Major Nathan G. Evans [7] of that regiment, and my brother, who was on staff duty with Colonel Richard H. Anderson,[8] then in command of Sullivan's Island, was a member of the mess at headquarters. I accepted gratefully and went with him.

When we got to headquarters on the Island I found my brother had been sent on some special duty by Colonel Anderson, who kindly invited me to stay with the mess till he got back. I also met Barnard E. Bee [9] who was lieutenant colonel of the regiment and Major Dunovant [10] who was one of the majors, Evans being the other. They were all very kind to me, especially Colonel Bee and Major Evans. Colonel Bee was a native of Pendleton, S.C., and had been a schoolmate of two of my uncles, my grandfather Langdon Cheves [11] having his summer home there.

I told Bee of my desire to get to Morris Island and he promised to arrange it if I wanted to go after seeing my brother Charles (Charles was older than William and when the war began was a civil engineer and working in Mississippi). My oldest brother Langdon was a planter near Pine Bluff on the Arkansas River. They both came home as soon as they heard of the State's Secession, Charles being at once commissioned in the first regulars and Langdon joining Colonel Maxcy Gregg as a volunteer aide.

Next day my brother Charles came in and soon after Colonel Bee, having had a talk with him, asked me if I would like to stay with them. He took me in to Colonel Anderson, who said he needed an aide, and would keep me as a volunteer if I could get a horse and would, if things suited, try to get me a commission. I gladly accepted and went on duty at once, living as a member of the mess till the bombardment of Fort Sumter.

Colonel Bee was especially kind to me and I always thought that he would have been one of the leading men in our army if he had lived. He was killed at Manassas in the first engagement. He had an enormous pointer to which he was devoted and the dog took a great fancy to me, which, I think, made Colonel Bee think well of me. When, ten days after the bombardment of Fort Sumter, he was ordered to Virginia, he left the dog with me, telling me that if anything happened to him I was to have the dog. I kept it until I was ordered to Virginia in July [12] the day after I had commanded a section of artillery at Bee's funeral—he having been killed on the 21 of July.

Soon after Colonel Bee left I was appointed to a lieutenancy in the battalion of regular artillery and was assigned to Company A [13] (Captain Ransom Calhoun [14]). The company was sent as a garrison to Fort Sumter, where it stayed some weeks; then it went to Charleston to organize as a light battery and was stationed in the grounds of the Arsenal (now Porter's school), where it stayed till the first of August, drilling. Soon after the funeral of Bee and Bartow [15] (of Georgia) it went by rail to Richmond, stopping there some six weeks when it was sent to Manassas Junction and later to Fairfax, where the army headquarters had been established.

About the first of December the company was ordered to return to Charleston to rejoin the battalion, which was to be increased to a regiment, of which Captain Calhoun became colonel. As I was not willing to go back, I resigned and was about to join a cavalry company from South Carolina when General Joseph E. Johnston [16] invited me to serve on his staff as a volunteer aide until something turned up. I stayed with him in this capacity till General Gustavus Smith [17] came up to take command of the wing of the army which General Johnston had brought from the Valley to the Battle of Manassas. When General Smith arrived he offered me a position on his staff,[18] at General Johnston's request, and I went on duty as assistant to Colonel Horace Randal,[19] his inspector general.

At this time General Johnston took command of the whole army, which consisted of his old Valley wing, Beauregard's [20] troops and the cavalry under Stuart,[21] although the first two kept their separate organizations until the army was reorganized in the winter of '61–'62.[22] General Johnston was at that time regarded by many as the coming soldier of the Confederacy. He was an ideal soldier, in the prime of a vigorous life, about 47 or 48 years old, rather undersized, but the most soldierly looking man in the army.[23] Very erect, he was a dashing horseman, with a rather stern, but handsome face, which could light up as brilliantly and look as kindly as it seemed possible for a face to look, yet it could change as suddenly to as stern and menacing expression as any face ever could. It was a true index to his character, which was as affectionate and warmhearted, but as quick and passionate, as any I ever met; yet his passion, which was sometimes of unseemly violence, was always as quickly followed by regret and acknowledgment so hearty and full that one could never

harbor resentment against as true and right-minded a gentleman as ever lived.

No one in the Confederate War, unless it were McClellan [24]
of the Union Army, can be compared with General Johnston
as an organizer of an army. He would in the European army
organization have been an ideal Quartermaster and Chief
of Staff, but was apt to wait too long in the effort to make
his preparations perfect and so lose opportunities, never to
be regained. As a soldier he will always rank high, though he
never achieved great results, attributable to some extent to
his relations with President Davis, who was of too impatient
and arbitrary a nature to handle as quick and impatient a
lieutenant as General Johnston.

Mr. Davis was a great man and as pure a patriot as the
South had, but unfortunately he had been a soldier by education. In the Mexican War he was in command of a regiment
and was one of the most brilliant soldiers of the war. Interested too much in details, he undertook to manage campaigns
as a soldier from his office in Richmond, instead of leaving
them to his generals, whom he would hold responsible for
results. General Johnston, on the other hand, resented this
constant interference, and never realized that the President
was often unable to give him the assistance he needed,
because Mr. Davis, too, was hampered, as all leaders have
ever been. He had the opposition of the aspiring politicians,
some of whom thought that they should have had the presidency, while others were preparing as future presidents. None
knew a surer way than to hamper and thwart the man they
thought in their path, and so fighting the incumbent wrecked
the Confederacy.

All leaders when chosen had suffered this when contending
for the existence of their countries. Few except Washington
and Lee have ever been able to shut their eyes and, what
is harder still, their mouths, to give their whole minds and
bodies to doing the best they could with such means as they

had and against the difficulties thrown in their way by those who would wear the lion's skin before the beast was slain. Neither Johnston nor Davis was of this kind, their first and last impulse being always to strike back.[25]

Mr. Davis saw too vividly the political necessity for action, but could not understand from his office in Richmond the insuperable difficulties, which were often thrown in the way by apparently unimportant details. He could not understand, when at the Battle of Manassas the Union Army had poured, a panic-stricken mob, back to Washington, why our victorious army could not follow them, to end the war, and eat and rest afterwards.[26] General Johnston, on the other hand, could not see that it was possible to give his men a few hours rest and a hurried feed, and to get to Washington for a complete victory and a long rest. Instead he went to work to replenish his stores, reorganize his broken organization and repair his transportation. So, halting between the two opinions, nothing was done; while the North, thoroughly humiliated but with her resources scarcely impaired, was fully and roughly aroused, and proceeded to lay the foundation of the enormous organization, which, although defeated on an hundred fields, slowly and surely wore the South down. When the end came and some thirty-odd thousand Confederate soldiers, teamsters and camp-followers laid down their arms, it was in front of a thoroughly equipped Union Army which was four times the size of that in 1861. General Gibbon,[27] the head of their commission at Appomattox, told me that they had no more only because they reported they could not use them to advantage as they had enough already.

Chapter 2

With General Johnston

GENERAL SMITH, on whose staff I went, was a graduate of West Point who had served with some distinction as a lieutenant of engineers in the Mexican War. Soon after its close he resigned and went to New York, where, when the war began, he had served for several years as street commissioner with great credit. For some reason he came South with a wonderful military reputation and was at once appointed major general, being the first to hold that rank,[1] and was sent to take command of Johnston's Army of the Valley. Beauregard had been promoted to the rank of general soon after Manassas.[2]

General Smith had imperfectly recovered from a stroke of paralysis, which had detained him for several months on his way South. It is probable that he was prevented by that attack from fulfilling the expectations of his friends, as he never rendered service to justify his reputation, though he certainly was a gallant gentleman of high intelligence and courage. He was second in command to General Johnston at Seven Pines and succeeded to the command when Johnston fell, severely wounded, in that fight. But he had a second stroke

of paralysis the night after the battle and was succeeded by
General Lee.[3]

My chief on General Smith's staff was Colonel Horace
Randal, in some respects the most remarkable man I met
during the war. He was, when I first met him, a year or two
under thirty, of a handsome carriage, and a most remarkable
horseman. He never spared his horse, but rode always at half
speed, day or night. I have seen his horse go down with him
many times, but he was always up as soon as the horse was,
on him and off again in the time that most men would take
to pick themselves up. He was a classmate of Stuart at West
Point, but had more physical dash than Stuart. His other
classmates, Hood [4] among them, always predicted that he
would be the cavalry leader of the war if he got a chance.

I was shown by someone (not Randal, for he was a most
diffident, modest man in speaking of himself) a report made
to the United States Congress by President Davis, when he
was Secretary of War, of a pursuit commanded by Randal,
of a murderous band of Indians. The report said that he had
for seven days pursued, making over eighty miles every
twenty-four hours, and, without losing a man or horse, had
overtaken and destroyed the entire band of Indians. General
Johnston had the greatest admiration and affection for him
and often gave him the most important duties and authority.
As he always took me with him, I got to know him very well.
I was very devoted to him and learned from him many things
which were of great service to me later. He was appointed
a brigadier general of cavalry during the winter of '61–'62,
sent to Texas, his native state, and unfortunately killed in a
skirmish soon after reaching there.[5]

On the day of the Battle of Leesburg,[6] known generally as
Ball's Bluff (which was fought about twenty miles from
Centerville, then army headquarters), General Johnston, as
soon as the news of the fighting reached him, ordered Randal
to go there as quickly as possible, giving him authority to

direct almost as he saw fit in his, General Johnston's, name. Randal went at once, taking me with him.

When we reached Leesburg it was almost dark and the fighting was over, having resulted in the complete defeat of the U. S. Troops. We found the army very excited over the results, but very indignant with Evans, who, the other officers freely said, had been two miles away in his tent and drunk, leaving the battle to be fought by the regiments individually, without an overall commander. The chief credit seemed to be divided equally between Colonels Burt [7] and Lomax,[8] both originally from Abbeville, one commanding a Mississippi and the other an Alabama regiment. Also, much credit was given Colonel Eppa Hunton,[9] commanding a Virginia regiment, and to Colonel Jenifer, who was in command of some cavalry.

Jenifer never reached higher rank than colonel, although he served creditably in all positions to which he was assigned. He was celebrated as a trainer of horses, to which animal he was devoted. During the war he rode a gray Arabian stallion, very beautiful and of almost human intelligence. It was hard to imagine anything a horse could do which this one would not do at Jenifer's command. I remember the first time I ever saw Jenifer, he was riding this horse past our camp at Manassas Junction. General George Crittenden,[10] a son of the Kentucky senator, was with me. (He was quite a friend of Captain Calhoun, with whom, I think he had been in West Point, and constantly visited him at our camp.) He had a remarkable amount of dry humor, and seeing Jenifer riding by, said, "There is Jenifer with his horse that has more sense than Jenifer, for Jenifer has taught him everything he ever knew and he had a lot of horse-sense to begin with." Jenifer was well known as the inventor of a military saddle much used at one time, but generally superseded by the McClellan, invented by General McClellan.[11]

Randal reported to General Johnston next day what he had found, that the entire credit of the victory was due

Colonels Burt, Lomax, Hunton and Jenifer. He further reported that Evans was said to have been drunk at his quarters over a mile from the battlefield, during the entire action, and that from his investigation there were good reasons to believe the report was correct.

General Johnston at once ordered Randal to prefer charges against Evans. (The report and order were given verbally, with me present because I had been with Randal at Leesburg and assisted him in his investigation.) Randal wrote immediately to Evans, who came the next day to the room where Randal and I worked. Randal was then at work on the charges, and Evans begged most earnestly to be helped. He said he had not been drunk, but had been quite sick and unfitted for active work; that he had been present during the greater part of the battle, although for a part of the time, when the fight was thought to be over and when it was really practically over, he had been resting on account of his physical disability. He appealed to me, too, for the sake of my brother Charles, who was his friend, to help him, if I could.

Finally Randal and I agreed to do all we could. We talked the matter over with General Smith, and he agreed, after some hesitation, to see what he could do with General Johnston. The evidence was by no means clear that Evans' account was not partly true, and we did not doubt his courage. The result was that General Johnston let the matter drop.[12]

At that time, headquarters were at Centerville, a little village five or six miles from Manassas Junction and about four miles from the battlefield. General Johnston's quarters were on the second floor—a very large hall with nice small rooms opening off it—of a building which had been a hotel. One of these he occupied and General Smith had another. Randal, who as I have said was inspector general of Smith's corps, had one at the other end of the hall, while the hall itself was occupied by General Smith's aide, John Lane (a son of Joe Lane of Oregon,[13] who was Vice Presidential candidate with Breckinridge,[14] when Lincoln was elected), James B. Washington,[15] General Johnston's aide, Wade Hampton, Jr.,[16] and myself.

General Johnston was then absolutely devoted to General Smith, who, he insisted, should be with him all the time. They had a common mess, and the personal staff of the two served each indiscriminately, although General Johnston used Randal more perhaps than any other staff officer. About the time Randal left for Texas L. Q. C. Lamar [17] came up and spent the rest of the winter, occupying Randal's room. He was nominally a volunteer on General Johnston's staff, though it was generally understood at headquarters that he was there to attempt to heal the breach (already giving trouble) between President Davis and General Johnston.

Lamar was sick for weeks, and during most of the time I occupied part of his room, as he seemed to like to have me look after him. I became very fond of him, and to the day of his death he was very devoted to me. He was a charming man, of the warmest heart and most pleasant to be with, though sometimes so absent-minded that he would for hours not seem to know of one's existence; then he would begin to talk most confidentially and charmingly of things either present or past. Many of his reminiscences of Mississippi or Washington life, if recorded, would be articles as brilliant as any ever written.

While sick and sometimes suffering greatly,[18] he was never for a moment impatient or complaining, and always grateful for the smallest attention. When late in the war I lost my arm, he came to see me as soon as he heard of my wound. When he came into my room in Richmond, where I was carried from the field, he knelt by my bed and threw his arms over me, burst into tears and said, "Would to God I had lost my life rather than this." He was led out, as he seemed utterly unable to control himself. I often saw him after the war, and he was always most cordial to me, but I only met him incidentally and never had very intimate association with him again.

The winter of '61–'62 was very quiet and uneventful, the army suffering chiefly and heavily from measles, which killed hundreds of soldiers.[19] There was one small fight at a place called Dranesville,[20] in which we got rather the worst of it, though it was a trifling affair. I was sent to get information and found the First Kentucky, which was the only body of Kentucky troops with our army, almost surrounded by the enemy. I was able to assist in getting them out of a very dangerous position by my knowledge of a blind road, which I had learned of on one of my trips with Randal.

While the army was idle at Centerville, almost every afternoon a party met at Longstreet's headquarters to practice jumping our horses. Each one who got a fall paid a forfeit which was spent for the entertainment and amusement of the club, of which Longstreet [21] was the head. He was a heavy man, weighing then not less than 200 pounds, and rode a large bay horse which had much the appearance of the finer express-wagon horses of today. He was a thoroughbred and the finest jumper in the army, carrying Longstreet over anything that any of the lightweights could take, and we never got a forfeit from Longstreet.

Another very fine horseman was General Field,[22] an old army officer, who rose to the rank of major general and received the command of Hood's Division, when Hood was sent to the Army of the West. He too, was a large man and was always well mounted, The one who generally did best was Major Manning [23] of Longstreet's staff, a little man, weighing not over 100 pounds. He was from Mississippi and always had a fine mount. But my brother, Alexander C. Haskell, who was then on General Gregg's staff, came one evening and was said to have done the finest riding ever seen at the meetings. I was not there, but I have always thought he was the finest horseman I ever saw.

General Johnston's elder brother, Beverley,[24] spent much of the winter at headquarters. He was an old bachelor, very choleric and disputatious, too fond of his toddy, and on one occasion when he had taken too much he visited the jumping club on a beautiful, small, brown horse, one of the favorites of the General. The old gentleman, who was about five feet, seven, and weighed over two hundred, insisted on trying the jumps, at which he and the pony came down, most disastrously to his nose and the pony's knees. General Johnston was so indignant that it had quite a dampening effect on the jumping, which was soon ended by the opening of the spring campaign.

At the headquarters mess it was quite a favorite joke to encourage the old gentleman to take too much and at the next meal to ask General Johnston's opinion on some disputed quotation of poetry or historical fact, about both of which he was wonderfully well informed. No matter what his opinion was, his brother, who went in the mess by the name of Tige (because of the remarkable likeness he bore to a bulldog of that name, owned by a man at whose house General Johnston made his quarters for some time, and which, while refusing to have anything to do with anyone else, was devoted to Mr. Johnston), would at once take the opposite side, and after a very warm controversy, his respect for his older brother would compel the General to leave the table.

The General was furious and took quite a dislike to two members of the mess whom he suspected, but who really had nothing to do with it. I don't think he ever for an instant suspected the right man, Colonel Charles M. Fauntleroy,[25] a naval officer, who for a long time served on General Johnston's staff. He was a very clever man with an inveterate passion for practical joking. He made it a rule, even on the march, to shave and to cut his hair every morning, the latter being done by clipping every lock long enough to be caught between his fingers. He was a remarkably well read man, as a naval officer had seen much of the world, and was a most interesting talker.

He was an excessively ugly man and rather vain. He bitterly resented his nickname of Figurehead Fauntleroy, which stuck to him and was unmercifully pushed because he never missed a chance to play practical jokes, and seemed to enjoy them most when they were most painful to the victim.

During the winter at Centerville I met many men, afterwards noted for their services. Hood was stationed some twenty miles from headquarters in command of the 4th Texas. He came up almost every week to visit General Smith, who was related to him, and Randal, who was a connection by marriage and had been his close friend and roommate at West Point. Hood was at that time a tall, rawboned country-looking man, with little of the soldierly appearance that West Point often gave its graduates. He looked like a raw backwoodsman, dressed up in an ill-fitting uniform. He afterwards filled out and became quite a fine-looking man of good address. He soon made his mark and later would have been named by three-fourths of the army as the finest division commander in the army. His men were devoted to him and believed in him absolutely. There was no task too great or too dangerous for them to undertake if he led them, and he was as popular and as trusted by his officers as his men. He was an ideal commander of volunteers and of a division, but when he was put higher, he failed.

The division commander, who would probably have been put next to Hood, was A. P. Hill,[26] who that winter was colonel of the 13th Virginia. Hill was a very pleasant, attractive man, quite good looking and rather dandified in his dress, which was always a blue, blouse shirt of broadcloth, with very conspicuous insignia of his rank and a treble row of large gold buttons. He was a stylish horseman, always well mounted, and presented a very pleasing appearance. I don't think very much was expected of him beyond being a creditable soldier, but he was the next year appointed major general in command of the Light Division of Jackson's Corps, and made for himself and his command a brilliant reputation. When Jackson was killed, Hill was promoted to lieutenant general and placed in command of the 3rd Corps, which he commanded with great credit until he was killed at Petersburg, when our lines were broken just a few days before the end.

Toombs [27] of Georgia was with the army, too, in command of a brigade. He was a defeated candidate for the Presidency and was rather bitter over his defeat. He never doubted the success of the Confederacy, and was in the war, which he never hesitated to say would end with the campaign of '62, distinctly as an episode in his political career. He was a loud, boisterous man, with many attractive qualities and a brilliant, if disorderly, character and intellect. He had a great contempt for West Pointers and a great dislike for Mr. Davis.

Sometime in the winter of '61–'62, General Johnston sent me to Toombs' quarters near Centerville with a written order of arrest. I learned afterwards that Toombs and one of his colonels, Gartrell,[28] had got in a most unseemly dispute, that the matter had finally been settled by General Johnston, but that Toombs had violated General Johnston's decision in a most insubordinate manner and had refused to obey later, hence the order for his arrest.

When I got to Toombs' quarters, which were in a small farmhouse, I presented the order, which he received with a perfect torrent of blasphemous abuse. At the first pause I resented it very decidedly. He stopped a moment and at once said I was right. He then made a most ample and manly apology.

A violent storm, which suddenly broke, kept me for hours at his quarters, and I never spent a more interesting night. He went on with his apology, saying "Captain, I should not have given way, but it does gall me when I am oppressed by a little man like Johnston, whom a few months ago I could have made or ruined by a word, and who, as soon as this little

war is over and I go to the senate, will be so much below me
that my sense of magnanimity will forbid me getting even
with him. Now, I don't mind Davis. We will be on the same
ground, and, damn him, I can make him smart for what he
does. But it will be like hitting a child to go at Johnston" (and
he believed every word of it, too).

After he cooled down, he talked for hours of Washington
life and men, and gave the most brilliant and vivid picture of
it. It was intensely interesting and lifelike. I saw a good deal
of him afterwards and always liked him greatly. He was no
soldier and had no business in the army, but he took good
care of his men and did the best he could. He was deserving
of much more credit than some who have a higher name in
history for their war record.

I saw a good deal, too, of Ewell,[29] who was a queer
character, very eccentric, but upright, brave and devoted. He
had no very high talent, but he did all that a man of courage
and moderate capacity could. Early,[30] who was his subordinate and successor, was equally queer and brave, a man of
more ability than Ewell, but not near so good a soldier. He
posed too much and always recalled to me Plato's speech to
Diogenes, that "he echoed his vanity by his rags." He had
quite a reputation as a division commander, but failed completely as a corps commander, especially in the Valley. He
continued to pose after the war and was very harsh in his
criticism of men who certainly did as good service as he did.
He denounced their errors mercilessly, while he and Beauregard were complacently earning enormous salaries by serving
as decoys for the Louisiana Lottery.

I met and saw frequently General Trimble [31] of Maryland,
who was often a guest of General Johnston of Centerville.
He was a charming old fellow, kindly and brave, but cranky.
He never would give anyone his proper military title, and
sometimes rather provoked General Johnston (who was inclined to be over-formal) by calling him always "Mr." John-

ston. Once when corrected he said, "Pshaw, this is only militia rank." Later in the war he was promoted to major general at Jackson's special request. The story was told that he hesitated to accept and said to Jackson that there were braver and abler men than he. But Jackson replied, "I am not promoting you for your ability, but because you will fight and will make your men fight."

The army was reorganized that winter, being formed into divisions with G. W. Smith, Longstreet, Jackson,[32] Holmes,[33] Huger,[34] and Kirby Smith [35] as major generals. None of these except for Jackson and Longstreet ever amounted to much, and gave some grounds for the charge, frequently made then and now, that we were handicapped by West Point. The Academy certainly gave us some great soldiers, but it also gave us some dummies, who were grievous stumbling-blocks in our way.

Perhaps Kirby Smith should also be expected from this list. He went West and the evidence as to his service is conflicting. He was a man of high character but mediocre ability. There was so much less fighting in the Trans-Mississippi area, that, like the one-eyed man in the country of the blind, anyone who was there was a great leader, and heroes were almost as cheaply made as in the Cuban war.

Stuart was another already noted man who was frequently at headquarters. He was a remarkable mixture of a green, boyish, undeveloped man, and a shrewd man of business and a strong leader. To hear him talk no one would think that he could ever be anything more than a dashing leader of a very small command, with no dignity and much boastful vanity. But with all he was a shrewd, gallant commander.

He was at that time a man of something under thirty, about five feet, eleven inches in height, and weighing about 180 pounds. He was a good looking man, coarse in feature and figure, but powerful and enduring, of immense energy, and as coolly brave an individual as ever lived. He saw everything in battle utterly undisturbed by the danger, and was quick to take advantage of anything that turned up, but was without the broad view that would foresee the results of any great move. His favorite companions were more or less buffoons, a part he, himself, greatly affected. Yet when he fell mortally wounded and died after many hours of fearful suffering, the man who the day before was singing minstrel songs with Sweeney's [36] banjo with apparently no higher desire in the world died bravely and uncomplainingly, making a glorious end of a very varied life.

I happened to be on duty one winter in Richmond, while recovering from a wound which unfitted me for field service, and was a regular attendant at St. Paul's church. No Sunday passed that Stuart, who was in camp near Richmond, failed to come in about ten minutes after services began. He would stalk down the aisle to a seat near the front, with his spurs jingling and swinging his cavalier's hat with an enormous plume, so that it was impossible to take him all in. Yet when he lay dying, his religion was a sure comfort to him, and when Jackson was wounded at Chancellorsville, he asked that Stuart be put in his place. Stuart filled it well and completed the victory which Jackson had planned and begun.

Jackson, who was already a very marked man, was often at headquarters, but would go at once to General Johnston's room, and when he came out, would go straight to his horse, never stopping to talk to anyone. He was a striking looking man, rather stiff and awkward in his movements, both on foot and on horseback, always rather shabby in his appearance and badly mounted, at a time when fine horses and stylish uniforms were the rule. He was always courteous, but beyond a salute he had rarely anything to say.

The first time I ever saw him was the morning we got to Centerville. I was sent by General Johnston to give some order to Colonel Jackson, then commanding the brigade which was afterwards known as the Stonewall Brigade. Riding down the road where I was told to find him, I met a poorly mounted officer in a very dingy blue uniform with a colonel's eagles on his shoulders.[37] I stopped and asked him if he could tell me where I could find Colonel Jackson. He looked at me rather quizzically and asked what I wanted with him. I told him that I had a message for the Colonel from General Johnston. "What is it?" he asked. I, never for a moment thinking he was Jackson, answered that it was for Colonel Jackson. "Well, you can give it to me," he said. I realized he was the man and gave it to him, though he never did say who he was. All he said was, "Tell General Johnston he shall have it." I was fresh from home, riding a very handsome horse, and all my equipment was brand new. He evidently took me for a rather cocky youngster, and was amused at my appearance.

Jackson's story is so well known as the most striking genius of the Army of Virginia, perhaps of that period, unless Forrest is entitled to that place,[38] that it seems useless to say anything about him. It has been the fashion to dwell on his peculiarities, till one who does not know something of him is apt to have an almost grotesque view of him, which does him an injustice. General Dick Taylor,[39] in his remarkably bright, but not very accurate book, *Destruction and Reconstruction,* writes very amusingly of Jackson, but no one reading it would form a just opinion of him. As I once heard a foreigner say, it gave him the idea of an eccentric man, who spent most of his life on his knees, praying and sucking lemons. It certainly gives no idea of a man of dignified deportment and fully worthy of his position. This he certainly was. I have been close to him many times, though I only knew him well enough to speak to him, but I never saw him praying or sucking lemons.

Once at Fredericksburg [40] I sat near him for some time on Telegraph Hill, where General Lee took his position during most of the battle. Jackson was sitting under a tree, reading a small book, which was probably a Testament, but every other time I saw him he was a busy, preoccupied man. His religion was too real a thing with him for him ever to make a show of it. He was as far above posing as any man who ever was conspicuous, the very highest type of Puritan.

A very remarkable incident about Jackson is the way that he got his name of Stonewall. Almost universally it is believed that Bee, in exhorting his brigade at Manassas, called to them admiringly to look at Jackson's men standing like a stone wall. Major Rhett,[41] who was General Johnston's Chief of Staff and a classmate of Bee and Jackson at West Point, was with Bee from soon after he was shot till he died. He told me often, as did General W. H. C. Whiting,[42] that the fact was that Bee said that his and Bartow's brigades were being hard pressed, that Jackson refused to move to their relief, and that he (Bee) in a passionate expression of anger denounced Jackson for standing like a stone wall and allowing them to be sacrificed.

This was confirmed to me repeatedly during the war and after by James Hill,[43] Bee's brother-in-law and aide-de-camp, who was with him when he fell. Hill said Bee was angry and excited when the fight was going on, and bitterly denounced Jackson for refusing to move. That this is the true story of Bee's connection, I have no doubt, as I heard it confirmed by more than one who was present at Bee's deathbed (he died in a house at Manassas Junction, four miles from the battle-field), but I am equally confident that Jackson acted from no unworthy motive. He was not only a great man, but one of the sternest Puritan nature, who would come as near as any man could to doing what he thought best, absolutely, regardless of whom it helped or hurt. And he did what he thought best from a military point of view; he certainly never doubted that he was right and the man who differed was wrong. I have not a doubt that this was the reason for the difference between him and Bee. I give the story only to show how remarkably things can be distorted afterwards.[44]

I can never be a blind admirer of Jackson. No man as

positive as he was can ever hope to escape grievous errors.
No excuse has ever been made which can justify him on the
26th of June, 1862, when he lay in comparatively easy striking
distance of Beaver Dam Creek. There thousands of our men
were killed and wounded in an attack which General Lee
made in the confident expectation that Jackson would simul-
taneously attack in the flank and rear of the enemy. When
he did move the next morning, the enemy retreated precipi-
tately without resistance; but until he did make such a move,
they could have repulsed General Lee's whole army indefi-
nitely. Nor can one overlook the fact that, according to General
Lee's report of the next day's fight (Cold Harbor or Gaines's
Mill, as it is known), Jackson failed to make the attack, as
ordered, and Longstreet, who expected to make a heavy
demonstration only, changed it to a resolute attack which
gained the day.[45]

Many said that Jackson thought it was time for his troops,
in view of the heavy service they had done, to have a rest
and to let others do the principal fighting, and he has been
charged repeatedly with being responsible for McClellan's
escape two days after Gaines's Mill, when he was resting his
men and McClellan passed by across a little creek and expos-
ing his flank for hours, only a mile away.[46] No one, however,
questions Jackson's genius or his devotion. His campaign in
the Valley [47] will no doubt rank as the most brilliant work
of the Army of Northern Virginia, and should, in my opinion,
rank next to if not even with Napoleon's greatest accomplish-
ments. His services at Chancellorsville,[48] as second in command, show that he could freely give all he had to his leader,
when that leader had his entire confidence, while his fight
at Second Manassas,[49] devoting his whole command to apparent annihilation till Longstreet could get up, was as sub-
lime as the Spartans at Thermopylae. As a subordinate he
never showed at his best except in these two instances. It was
as an independent commander, unhampered except by general

instructions, charged only to gain a certain thing, that he rose highest. Then, on more than one occasion, when apparently hopelessly overwhelmed, he wrested complete triumph from apparently hopeless defeat by the force of his genius and his devotion.

Whether Jackson had the capacity to have taken the position of Commander in Chief is a question that will never be settled. Many of his admirers think he would. I cannot think so. There is no doubt that he did wonders with the scant material he had. There is no doubt, also, that he wore it out very fast and did not seem to provide in his campaigns for any sufficient reserve for the next and the question is if he had had control of all the resources of the country, scant as they were, could he have made them last to the end. To my mind, General Lee was the only commander on either side who came near to getting all out of his resources that could be done without exhausting them and leaving nothing for the next step. Some had genius to husband their resources and effect little. He alone would risk all when necessary, strike quick and run great dangers when he thought the end justified the risk, but he always kept a clear view of the next step or the next campaign.

Grant, who will rank as the greatest leader on the other side, had none of Jackson's genius and used his resources with either absolute blindness or with blind confidence in them. With Jackson's means and no more, he would have begun and ended in one campaign, and never been heard of again. Sherman had, evidently, more of the political capacity, which would have, perhaps, made him foresee difficulties, but he had not the high character or devotion which gave Lee and Jackson their prominence. He was a strong man but a shifty politician, not a statesman or a devoted patriot.[50]

Grant had much more of devotion and resolution, but he also lacked the high character which Lee and Jackson had, as evidenced by his lamentable career, when as President he was the tool of tricky or selfish politicians and, later, the catspaw of small Wall Street swindlers, to whom he blindly surrendered his name and reputation to trade on.

But all this is outside the story which I proposed to be a personal narrative of my experiences. Being thus led off into speculation makes me think that my objection to writing of the war is perhaps wiser than I thought. Still it need never see the light, and as I have written it I will let it stand.

Chapter 3

The Richmond-Washington Line

GENERAL JOHNSTON made much of my services in the affair at Leesburg, and secured my commission as major on the staff.[1] It was in the Commissary Department, though I did not do any service in that department till later, and even then it was only nominal, though it came very near costing me dearly. I, like most others who had not had measles, caught them and was quite ill. The day I first was well enough, I had news from Manassas Junction which rendered it important for me, as acting inspector, to go there. I started, not knowing that owing to recent rains the streams were all full. As I was leaving I met Colonel Wade Hampton,[2] who was camped at Occoquan[3] and had been up to see General Johnston. We rode together, going by way of Mitchell's Ford on Bull Run, instead of by the bridge route. When we reached the Bull Run we found it a raging torrent, far out of its banks. Colonel Hampton said that we had better swim across, rather than to go a long way down over a very bad road to the bridge. He told me to show him the way, as I was familiar with the road.

I did not like it, as I had had but little experience in swimming a horse and the current was very strong. But I was ashamed to admit it, and rode in to swim straight across. The

26

result was that my horse was swept below the landing place. I had a hard struggle for a long time to get out, but did so finally, utterly exhausted and soaking wet from head to foot, with the weather far below freezing.

When I got to the Junction my clothes were frozen stiff and I was in a shaking chill. Major Fisher [4] of Louisiana was post quartermaster. He took me in charge, got me in hot blankets at once, gave me hot stimulants, and put servants to rubbing me. This, the doctors said, probably saved my life, but could not save me from a sharp attack of pneumonia, through which I was devotedly nursed by Drs. Gaillard [*] and Fauntleroy,[5] surgeons of Generals Smith and Johnston, respectively.

When I got over my pneumonia I was a sufferer from bronchitis till the doctors ordered me off and I started home. When I got to Petersburg, the train south was only flatcars, all loaded with soldiers. I got a place on one with my valise for a pillow, as I was soon very sick. When we got to Weldon, then the most desolate station in the South, I was partly delirious, but I had sense enough to go to the hotel, where I was told very roughly that they had no room and that they did not want sick men anyhow. I went into the baggage room and lay down on the floor, soon becoming entirely delirious. Here I was found by Major Prioleau Hamilton [6] of South Carolina, who had me taken to his room and telegraphed to my brother William, who was with his regiment at Suffolk.

Major Hamilton stayed with me until the second day after, when my brother came up with Dr. Powell,[8] afterwards medical director of Hill's Corps, who had known me as a

---

[*] Dr. Gaillard, when General Johnston was shot down at Seven Pines, went to his assistance and while dressing his wound was himself severely wounded, losing his arm. After the war he was professor in the Medical College at Louisville, Kentucky, later going to New York, where he edited a medical journal. After his death, the journal was successfully conducted by his widow, who was Miss Mary Gibson, a daughter of Dr. Charles Bell Gibson of Richmond, the leading surgeon of the Confederacy.[7]

student in the South Carolina College. Dr. Powell had me moved to a private house and remained with me until my father and mother got on from home. They brought with them our family physician, Dr. Mabry, who stayed with me until I was well enough to be taken home. There I stayed until well enough to return, when I rejoined the army on its way from the Peninsula to Richmond.

The latter part of the winter of '61–'62 was quiet and un-eventful. With the Spring came the end of the term of enlist-ment of many of the soldiers. Most of them went home to visit their families. The majority soon re-enlisted but often in new commands; some did not re-enlist at all, others did much later. Many of the regiments reorganized with new officers.[9] The general effect was to break up very much the organization of the army. Partly owing to this and partly to the fact that the enemy gave signs of moving against us by the waterways, our army fell back on Richmond.[10]

When I got back to the army it was about 20 miles below Richmond, so I know nothing of the campaign except that part which is history. It had been augmented by the army which had been on the Peninsula and by troops from the South, and took an extended line from the James River to Chickahominy and the Brook Turnpike, an average distance of about ten miles from Richmond. General G. W. Smith was given command of the left wing of the army, with consider-able additions to his division. Several of his staff, I among the number, stayed with the staff of the division, which was then commanded by General D. R. Jones,[11] a native of South Carolina and a West Pointer. He was a pleasant gentleman and a brave soldier, but never was distinguished. He was quite an invalid and died in the winter of '62–'63. His wife was a niece of President Taylor, which made him more prominent, as President Davis was devoted to any kin of his first wife, who was President Taylor's daughter.

General Jones ordered me to assume charge of the commissariat though there was nothing for me to do. But he was devoted to red tape, and to give my position the appearance of having something to do he required all brigade commanders to come to me to get orders for everything. I had consequently to receipt to the Chief Commissary of the army for the supplies of some 12,000 men. In a very short time I was charged with hundreds of thousands of dollars of provisions of all kinds, though I never saw any of them except perhaps when I met a drove of cattle or wagon-loads of flour and groceries. I was as ignorant of business as most boys who have had no experience, and had a clerk detailed to keep accounts and care for receipts. When not long after I was severely wounded he robbed me of everything he fancied and scattered the receipts, so that when I got well I found I was short hundreds of thousands of dollars.

The brigade commissaries resented greatly having to ride several miles every day to get orders from me for their supplies, none so much as Major R. J. Moses,[12] commissary of Toombs' Brigade. He resented it and never ceased to do so, and directed his feeling at me, who was as much opposed to it as he was. He was when the war began, a prominent lawyer of Columbus, Georgia, having been counsel for the owners and crew of the *Wanderer*,[13] which just before the war undertook to bring a cargo of slaves from Africa but was captured.

Moses was a most witty and amusing man, a great friend of mine after I ceased to be his superior officer. He it was who first found the lamentable state of my accounts, and at once set himself to work to straighten them out. He worked at it for weeks, getting where possible, duplicate receipts. When after he had gotten all that were possible I was still behind a great many thousands of dollars for things I had neither seen nor touched, he prepared a bill relieving me, and with General Toombs' assistance had it passed. When I was sufficiently recovered to be taken home, he brought it to me. He was soon after selected by Longstreet to be chief commissary of his corps, and was known as one of the best, if not the best officer in his department. I always felt grateful affection for him, and we were as close friends as a boy and a man past middle age could well be.

I was with General Smith intermittently until the battle of the Seven Pines.[14] The evening of the battle I went to where the fighting was going on, and was sent by General Smith to carry an order to one of the brigade commanders. In doing so I got my horse injured so that I had to walk several miles to camp in the rain. I had been ailing for some two or three weeks, and this walk with the wetting I got brought on an attack of fever which had not left me when the Seven Days' battles began, though I had been out a good deal on duty for General Jones. I went to the battlefield at Mechanicsville [15] and got back very sick late that night. Next morning the whole staff went out, leaving me sick in camp, and firing began spasmodically along the line. I got the doctor to give me some opium pills, and I rode to the front, taking them frequently, as I was suffering very much.

I was riding a very remarkable horse which I had bought the winter before from General Turner Ashby,[16] who said that it was the most unusual horse he had ever owned. It was worthless to him with his regiment, as at the rattle of arms when drilling it would at once bolt and run till it was tired out. The result was that Ashby was liable to be carried away from his men at a most critical time. The horse was a medium-sized bay, with black legs and black stripe as large as a zebra's down its back. It never tired, never seemed to fear anything, and would swim, which it always seemed to like, with its body high out of the water. It would jump anything it was put at and, when bolting, anything that came in its way, sometimes going at things impossible to jump and coming down disastrously. As a staff officer, I could ride it without bad results, although it often ran away with me and had me in rather awkward places. But I was young enough to take the risk.

When I reached the front [17] I found General Magruder,[18] who was the Corps Commander, with General Jones sitting on their horses, looking across to the North side of the Chickahominy in some excitement. As I came near I heard a staff officer say, "There is a horse that can do it." I found that he referred to my horse, and that he meant, could swim the Chickahominy, which was out of banks in a big freshet. From the hill where the generals were, they could see General Lee's army marching down the river hills, while the enemy were next to the river, behind the flank of General Lee's line. General Magruder thought they might be dangerous to that flank and wanted to send a warning to Lee.

I undertook to carry the message and going, as I thought, well above the Yankees rode in, soon getting into swimming water. As I got to where my horse could touch bottom, I saw a squad of some eight or ten of the enemy riding to head me off. They evidently thought I could not get away, and let me get into comparatively shallow water before ordering me to surrender. But my horse's great power and my light weight enabled me to escape them, though they got within a short distance of me and but for their excitement could readily have shot me. As it was they fired numbers of rounds without touching me, and I got away from them to reach General Lee.

He heard my message and told me to wait, as he might want to send some message back. He then forgot all about me, and I attached myself to General Longstreet whom I had known in our jumping club at Centerville. In the course of an hour or so I found myself in what General Longstreet always said was in his opinion the hottest musketry fight in history. Finally, all of his staff having been sent on messages, he told me to go and put General R. H. Anderson's brigade into action at a point he showed me.[19]

I went at once and found General Anderson (my former chief at Sullivan's Island who had come to the army in Virginia), and gave him the order. He sent me with a message to General Whiting, whom I met for the first time. He was a West Point officer, having graduated far ahead of his class in every branch taught there. He started his career with a prestige which he did not fully sustain, though he made a fine reputation. His friends, however, thought that he did not get the chances or the rank to which he was entitled. He was probably the finest engineer in the army, and would probably have done more brilliant service if kept on staff duty. But he was very ambitious and very brave, and the line of distinction was as a commander in the field. He asked me who I was, and when I told him that I was only accidentally with General Longstreet, he asked me to help him rally some scattered men. We got together several hundred, and he told me to move them forward to the right of his division, which was heavily engaged. He then went to another part of the line.

We pushed forward and soon came in front, quite near to the enemy, who were lying down behind a breastwork of timber and earth. On the way, I passed General Pickett,[20] who was standing by his horse in a deep small hollow, almost like a well, bewailing himself. He called to me to send him a litter as he was mortally wounded, but I had none and was busy with my men. He was very slightly wounded and perfectly able to take care of himself.

When we got close to the enemy's line, we found a great many men lying down. My men followed suit, and I set to work trying to push them in. I saw a stand of colors held upright by a color bearer who was lying flat on his face. I rode to him and jerked it out of his hands. He at once jumped up and demanded them back, saying in reply to my question that he would take them in if the colonel, and he pointed to him lying near, would go on.

I rode over to the colonel and punched him in the back

with the flag staff. He jumped up, but when I told him to take the colors and lead his men in, he set to shaking as if in a chill, and suddenly broke off in a run to the rear. I shifted the flag to my left hand and riding up to him, struck him on the head with my sword; but it turned and the flat of it struck him hard enough to knock him to his knees. He cried out but ran on some thirty yards, when he jumped in the air and fell, apparently dead.

Almost immediately after a ball struck my saddle, grazing my leg and going into my horse, which fell to his knees. He had, up to this time, been the best horse I ever saw in battle, the only effect of the firing being to steady him, though I thought he would be utterly unmanageable. I pulled him to his feet, and—not realizing that he fell from the shot—struck my spurs into him. When the spurs pricked him, though I am sure he was mortally wounded, he made one of his typical rushes and had me over the breastworks. But he was shot dead in the act of leaping, and I was lying under him among the enemy.

A captain, I think of a New York regiment, ran up to me and grabbing the flagstaff called out to me, "You damned little rebel, surrender." I held on and jerked him to me, striking at him at the same time with my sword, which was hung to my wrist by a sword knot. He at once jumped back and fired at me with his pistol, cursing me all the time and tugging at the flagstaff. I kept jerking it back and striking at him with my sword, while at the same time struggling to get from under my dead horse, which was lying on my legs.

One ball from the pistol struck the star of my collar and burned my neck like fire, while another struck my little finger, breaking it and smashing a seal ring which I wore. Another just grazed my leg, but that one felt like a double-heated, hot iron, and made me struggle so that I found myself free from my horse and on my feet.

Our troops by this time were pouring in and the Yankees

running, my opponent among them. But he was a little too late, and I caught up with him. I cut down on him with both hands, expecting to split him, as we used to read of in novels, but my sword bounced off, knocking him to his knees. He rose and turned, facing me with his pistol in his hand. I never doubted but that he was about to shoot again and ran him through. He lived only a few minutes, trying to say something. I told him that I would send his effects to his people, which was apparently what he was trying to ask.

As soon as I could, I started to re-form the men I had been leading. While I was doing this, General Hood came from my left. He was re-forming his brigade. He spoke to me, offering to help me, as I was very bloody. When I told him I was not seriously hurt, he said that he was about to charge the battery which was sweeping the level beyond the ravine, where we had just broken the enemy's first line, and suggested that I join my men to his right.

I did so, and we charged across the plateau about four or five hundred feet. When I got within a few feet of the guns, I marked a gunner fixing his lanyard into the friction primer. I made a run to cut him down before he could fire, but he was too quick. When I was not over ten feet from the muzzle the gun went off. The shot struck my right arm, crushing it and tearing it off at the shoulder. When it hit me, it seemed to knock me up in the air and spin me around two or three times, though I suppose that was imaginary, and then dashed me down with a force that knocked all the breath out of me.

When I came to, I found my arm wrapped around my sword blade in a most remarkable manner. I sat up, but almost immediately everything went dark, and I supposed I was dying. After some time I regained consciousness and unwound the fragments of my arm from my sword blade, which I got back into the scabbard. I succeeded in stuffing my arm into the breast of my coat, got to my feet and started to the rear, using the flagstaff as a support. As I got back to the edge of the ravine from which we had started our charge I heard my name and saw Bradfute Warwick of Richmond, lying with his shirt bosom torn open and a shot through the lungs. He was calling for help. I showed him that I could do nothing, but a moment after I saw a member of his regiment, whom I told to go to his assistance. He was sent home that night to Richmond, but his wound was mortal and he died a few days later. He was that day commanding the Fourth Texas, Hood's original regiment, of which he was lieutenant colonel.

Warwick was in Europe, where he had gone to complete his medical education, when Garibaldi was leading the Italians in their fight for independence. He had joined them as a volunteer, gaining considerable credit and the rank of major in the Italian army. He had visited Charleston immediately after the bombardment and surrender of Fort Sumter and had been my guest at the Fort for several days. He received me most hospitably when I went to Richmond, and we were quite good friends. He was a most gallant soldier, and would have won much distinction had he lived.[21]

Very soon after I passed Warwick I fell and could not get up. I was lying there expecting to die when General Whiting, riding by, saw me. He at once dismounted and gave me some whiskey from his flask. With the assistance of a straggler whom he called, he got me on his horse and accompanied me to where a field surgeon was helping the wounded and sending them to the hospital, farther back. The surgeon attended to my wound, bandaging it tightly to my side. Just then Colonel Upson [22] of Texas, a member of General Whiting's staff and after the war a member of Congress from Texas, came up, and General Whiting turned me over to him. The General then mounted his horse and rode back to the field.

In going out, Upson and I passed near where General Lee and his staff were sitting on their horses. Colonel Venable [23] of the staff had been a professor at the South Carolina College when the war began. He recognized me and rode up to see if he could be of help. This attracted the attention of the General, who rode up and asked what surgeon I wanted. I told him either Powell or Darby,[24] and he at once ordered one of his couriers to bring the first of these he could find. At the same time he ordered his private ambulance to be brought for me, and wrote a note to Dr. Gibson, the leading surgeon of Richmond, asking him to give me special care. About this time Dr. Darby arrived, but on examining my wound he told me I would not recover, and after doing what he could for my comfort, he told me goodby.*

Soon after the ambulance started to Richmond with me, it took up T. M. Logan [25] of the Hampton Legion. He was shot in the foot and rode with the driver on the front seat. While we were stopping for him Colonel D'Orsay Cullen,[26] Longstreet's medical director, rode up and hearing that I was in the ambulance got in to see me. He found me suffering greatly with cold, though it was a hot, summer day. I was suffering great pain too. He had me lifted up, and then wrapped me in a beautiful rug, one which Collie,[27] the great blockade-runner, had brought in and which Cullen prized highly. Then, telling me goodby most affectionately, he put some bitter powder in my mouth. He told me afterward that it was morphine enough to kill several men, and that he gave it to me to allow me to die easily, as I appeared to be in great suffering. He often said that my recovery from him was much more remarkable than my recovery from the wound.

We got to Richmond about two or three o'clock in the morning, and I was carried to the Spotswood Hotel, kept by a man named Hoenninger,[28] who in some way had become

* Dr. Darby was a relative who, when the war began, was practicing in Philadelphia. He came South and entered the army as a surgeon of Hampton's Legion. At the end of the war he was chief surgeon of Hood's Corps in the Western army. After the war he was professor of surgery in the New York College of Surgeons, but died not long after he took that position.

a protégé of General G. W. Smith and his wife. He was often at headquarters and claimed to be a member of General Smith's staff. He called himself colonel, though never even in hearing distance of a battle. He was always profuse in his invitations to all of the staff to come to his hotel if ever wounded. But when I got there he sent me word that to his great regret the hotel was full and he could not take me in. It was almost the only instance of which I ever heard of a wounded soldier being refused admission.

We then drove to Dr. Gibson's home on Franklin Street to deliver General Lee's note and to ask the doctor where I should go, i.e., to what hospital. While we were waiting at his door, Mr. Thomas Dudley [29] came up from the hospitals, where he had been at work all night as he always was when wounded men were being brought in. He asked who was in the ambulance, and at once had me carried into his house. He knew who I was, as his son Tom, afterwards Bishop of Kentucky, and my brother William were very intimate friends at the University of Virginia. To this I certainly owe my life, as I was cared for with a devotion equal to that I would have had at home, and had the attention of the most skillful surgeons of the Confederacy.

Dr. Middleton Michel of Charleston, although at that time recovering from a very severe attack of blood poisoning, which disabled his hand, was with me day and night and gave me the most devoted care. He was a distant family connection and a very skilled surgeon. He and Miss Ann Johnson, a step-daughter of Mr. Dudley, took entire charge of me. She was an invalid and a cripple, but a stronger, higher spirit never lived. She never showed a sign of physical weakness or suffering, and Dr. Gibson often said that he knew few surgeons he would prefer to her as an assistant, and no number of trained nurses could improve her work.

Mr. and Mrs. Dudley did all for me that my parents could have done. He was as noble, big-hearted a man as ever lived.

During the war he devoted his days to the support of his family and a house always full of guests, usually those who needed help, but no night when the wounded were coming in ever saw him at home until near daylight, his whole nights at such times being spent in serving the wounded.

After the end of the war I did not see Richmond for many years. But then every member of the family had passed away except Bishop Dudley, from whom I parted at Appomattox, where he was an assistant in the Commissary Department with the rank of major. I have never seen him but once since, when I met him as he was getting off a train and had a few minutes talk with him. As usual, he had a witty story to tell of a Boston philanthropist, who asked Bishop Wilmer [30] of Alabama (Tom Dudley's ideal) to tell him if Southerners really hitched negroes to the plow instead of mules. Bishop Wilmer replied by asking if the questioner knew the relative power to pull a plow. When he answered, ten to one in favor of the mules, the Bishop asked if he really thought any Southerner would be fool enough to put ten thousand dollars worth of negroes to doing the work of a hundred dollar mule. [31]

Chapter 4

North Carolina and Gettysburg

AFTER I got home from Richmond I had a long weary wait before I could get back to the army. I finally returned about the first of December, and spent the time at General Headquarters until the Battle of Fredericksburg on the 13th.[1] I was then a volunteer with General Lee, though I had almost nothing to do but to sit on Telegraph Hill, where he stood during most of the battle.

I was sent to order one command (Kershaw's[2] Brigade) in, and a piece of shell struck my coat-sleeve, which my tailor had sewed very firmly in my coat. As my horse jumped at the same time, I got about as hard a fall as I have ever had, and my shoulder, which had not healed, was so cut and bruised that it was weeks before I got over it.

When I got well I was ordered to North Carolina to organize the artillery and, incidentally, to command it, though I don't think anyone expected much to be done there.[3] But very soon after I got there, with headquarters at Goldsboro, Foster[4]—the commanding general of the Union troops—began to be active, and we had a good deal of fighting, though in a rather small way, until the next summer, when our army moved into Pennsylvania on the Gettysburg campaign.

The enemy had possession of almost all the coast of North Carolina, including New Bern, Beaufort, and the navigable streams on that part of the coast. General Smith, who had been in charge of the Department of Lower Virginia and North Carolina, gave up the command, and General French [5] succeeded him. French went to work organizing and training the men, but was shortly superseded by General D. H. Hill.[6] Hill was an old army officer, trained at West Point, but teaching when the war began. He was a man of considerable capacity and always seemed to go from choice into the most dangerous place he could find on the field. He was as earnest in his Puritan beliefs as was Stonewall Jackson, who was his brother-in-law, and greatly resembled Jackson in many other ways; perhaps he imitated him. He had a high and well deserved reputation as a hard fighter.

Hill was later promoted to the rank of a temporary lieutenant general under an act passed to permit men needed for immediate commands to have them with only temporary appointments. If as was true in some instances it was never sent in for confirmation, it would lapse. Hill's was such a case. For some reason his appointment was never sent to the Senate, and he returned to the rank of major general.[7]

Almost the first move Hill made was against New Bern.[8] He went down the south side of the river with two brigades and some cavalry, while General Johnston Pettigrew [9] moved down the other side with his brigade of full five thousand men, a few additional infantry, and four batteries. I went with General Pettigrew as directed.

He was a North Carolinian, though he was living in Charleston, practicing law with his uncle, James L. Petigru,[10] a celebrated lawyer, when the war began. His reputation for genius went back to his college days, and it was said that Maury,[11] the distinguished writer on tides and other marine matters, thought so highly of him that early in the war he wrote President Davis, urging Pettigrew's appointment as commander-in-chief of the Southern armies. Pettigrew had studied military science very earnestly, and spent some time in Europe trying to see active service, although I believe he had not been very successful. He was a singularly charming man, whose men were devoted to him and felt the most implicit confidence in him. I had never previously met him, but soon fell under the influence of his charm and was devoted to him ever after.

His was an ideal command, among his field officers being some dashing and brilliant men. Henry K. Burgwyn, Jr., was colonel of the 26th North Carolina Infantry. He was a most attractive person of about 24 or 25, with whom I became very intimate. Another man of brilliant promise was James K. Marshall, colonel of the 52nd North Carolina Infantry. He was a Virginian, a member of the family of Chief Justice Marshall, but was living in North Carolina when the war began. Both of these and Pettigrew's adjutant, Captain Colin Hughes, a most accomplished and gallant man, were killed in their first serious battle at Gettysburg. Others who were distinguished were Lieutenant Colonel Charles M. Steadman of the 44th North Carolina Infantry, Major John T. Jones of the 26th, and perhaps above all, Lieutenant Louis T. Young of Charleston, a devoted friend of Pettigrew, who sought no position which would remove him from his place as Pettigrew's aide, but in that was, next to Pettigrew, more considered than any man in the brigade and looked to in every emergency for directions by men and officers.

In his anxiety to get to his place on time and not having much experience in men's capacity to march, Pettigrew kept us going day and night, and got us within a short distance of Neuse River ahead of the wagons. As a result we were a day ahead of Hill on the other side, and were too hungry and exhausted to move to the attack. Fortunately, the enemy was thoroughly inexperienced, and though we lay for 28 hours in three or four miles of them, they never seemed to suspect trouble until we were actually on them at the end of that time.

They were occupying an earthwork on the bank of the river immediately opposite New Bern. About a quarter of a mile in front of them there was a seemingly impassable marsh, crossed by a causeway about a quarter of a mile long and only wide enough for a single farm wagon. Just at dawn on the second morning we dashed across this causeway with four batteries, supported by skirmishers and immediately followed by the infantry, which used the causeway and numerous small tracks made by cattle.

The enemy offered no opposition, being terror-stricken. We at once opened fire from the guns, and as the skirmishers ran in close to the fort, a white flag was hung out. We stopped firing to receive a deputation, whereupon the officer second in command came out and appealed to Pettigrew to grant a truce for an hour, so that he might communicate with his commanding officer in New Bern. (We learned afterwards that the commander of the fort was actually panic-stricken and that the officers we saw had shut him up so that he could not surrender.) Pettigrew went through the form of consulting Young and me, who were with him, but paid little attention to our strong urgency that he should refuse, and granted the time asked for.

Pettigrew afterwards explained that he felt that they were at his mercy, and he did not want to have the unnecessary loss of a life on his conscience. For that reason he gave the asked-for truce. But long before the time was out, we could see the smoke of the enemy's gunboats coming up the river, and we left under the heavy fire of ten and fifteen inch guns, losing ten times as many men as would have been killed, even had the garrison attempted to resist our advance.

Hill failed, too, on his side, and the whole move was without any good results. It seemed hard to realize that a man of Pettigrew's force and of the coolest, personal bravery could have made so grave a mistake, but he was a very tender-hearted, sensitive man, who shrank from the danger and suf-fering to others, of which he seemed careless for himself. His only battle before this was Seven Pines, where he was desperately wounded and fell into the hands of the enemy.[12]

After this fiasco we moved to a line farther back, and finally placed batteries in front of Washington, North Carolina, and at a point called Fort Hill.[13] There the enemy fleet in the Pamlico River had the first calliope I had ever heard. Every day after dinner they would play it for a while and then shell our position for an hour or two. They never did any real harm; it was almost as if it were done for an evening's entertainment.

I think the only man ever struck was Colonel Wharton Green [14] of Hill's staff. He was hit by a fragment of shell about four or five inches square, which had flown in from a shell bursting in the rear of the earthwork. He was a very thin man then, and when it hit him he doubled back, his head going near to his heels. It fortunately struck him, as General Hill called attention to, on the only spot which was sufficiently covered to protect his bones. Beyond making riding uncomfortable for a few days, it did him no harm.

Immediately in front of Washington, the firing was some-times severe, but it did little harm. The enemy had several heavily armed gunboats, that is, they had heavy guns, but they were wooden boats only. They lay close to the bridge and were almost safe. But two English cannon and shells were sent to me, and one day after we received these guns one of the boats ventured into the open. Before the crew found their danger we sank it, and they had to tumble off into the water. The hull gave us a target until we left there, as the enemy were always tinkering at the wreck with our men shooting at them. It was our chief occupation and amuse-ment, but there was little harm done.

The main entrance to Washington was over a long causeway

through a swamp. We had a squadron of cavalry, whose major was satisfied that he was a great partisan leader. He persuaded General Hill that if he would get a piece of the artillery in the night to the end of the causeway, he could sink the whole fleet of gunboats, which would be within 600 yards.

General Hill was much excited over the suggestion and sent for me to carry it out. I examined the place carefully with its discoverer, and found that the river-banks were so high that we could see nothing but the smokestacks of the gunboats, while an enemy land battery of heavy guns, a little over a quarter of a mile opposite, commanded the position completely.

General Hill was very dissatisfied by my report, and in a day or so sent for me. He said that the Major would build a protection for the gun, and all I would have to do would be to furnish the gun and a detachment. I told him I would not do it except on his written order, which he finally gave me. I handed him a written protest with a request to be relieved from his department. That night the Major reported his fort finished, and I took a gun down (a 12-pounder, the heaviest we had), put it into position, and as ordered opened fire at daylight, although General Hill had written me to come to his quarters before we began firing.

We did little harm, but finally did knock the top off a smokestack. Then the enemy, having gotten ready, opened on us with their battery. Our work was built, as I soon found, of timbers fished out of a creek which ran close to its base. The very first shot that struck it full knocked it all to pieces, killing several of the men who were behind it and completely disabling the whole thing. I, fortunately, was standing on top to be able to see, and the shot that killed the men pitched me into a slimy creek, but did me no material harm. The enemy apparently recognized our helplessness and ceased firing on us, allowing us to take out our dead and wounded unmolested.

I went back to camp, and very soon General Hill came to see me. When he heard that practically all the men had been killed or wounded, he went into ecstasies over what he insisted was a grand feat. He seemed utterly unable to see the terrible side of sacrificing eight or ten men for nothing. I saw as little as possible of him after this, and not long after left for the Army of Virginia.

Soon after this incident we abandoned the siege of Washington and fell back to our former line. There was, however, one old fashioned thirty-pounder on a siege carriage that I could get no transportation for. I therefore dismounted it, burned the carriage, and heating the gun red hot, had it battered out of shape with sledge hammers. When General Hill heard of this, he said that the army was disgraced, and he would get that gun out if it cost a hundred lives. He formed his lines on the crest of a hill, where they were exposed to fire from the guns on the boats, and sent parties out to gather mules and oxen.

Few men were hurt, but they were much distressed and annoyed by the shells falling among them. Finally, Generals Pettigrew and Daniel [15] asked me to go with them to remonstrate with General Hill against keeping the men so uselessly exposed. Pettigrew was the spokesman. General Hill heard him, and then, in the most natural and inoffensive tone, said, "General Pettigrew, if you do not like to stay under fire, turn your command to Colonel Leventhorpe." [16] Pettigrew, utterly shocked, drew off, and Daniel and I, resenting the insult, replied strongly. But General Hill calmly disavowed all intention of being offensive. He just repeated that all he had said was that if Pettigrew did not like it, he could turn over his command.

General Hill was eccentric to the verge of wrongheadedness. He constantly came out with the most extraordinary manifestoes. One offered a reward to anyone who would ever find him a dead cavalryman with his spurs on, though he must have known that our cavalry compared favorably with any of our troops as fighters. Frequently, during the siege of Washington, he would come to the guns and tell me that he believed Foster, the commander of the Yankees, lived at a part of town which he would point out and ask me to throw shells there. As we were not shelling the town, and it would be impossible to throw shells in it and not hit non-combatants, I always declined. He never gave me positive orders, though he was much dissatisfied that I would not do as he suggested. But he certainly was a good fighter and had much merit, though some extraordinary, queer notions.

Soon after this I was ordered to join Longstreet at Culpeper.[17] He applied for me while he was at Suffolk,[18] and I was ordered direct by the War Department. After I arrived at Culpeper I was assigned to a battalion which had been with Hood for some time. It had been commanded by Major Winston Henry,[19] who had applied for transfer to the Western Army. He had served as first lieutenant of Pelham's battery of horse artillery and afterwards as captain—on Pelham's promotion—until he was made chief of artillery of Hood's Division. He was a West Pointer and a very gallant man. He greatly distinguished himself at Fredericksburg in immediate command of a gun, for the work of which General Lee made a most enthusiastic report of Pelham's conduct. This was deserved, as Pelham,[20] being the senior officer, was entitled to the credit, but he always said that he would not have kept the gun there, had it not been for Henry's encouragement and approval.

Henry was my junior in date of commission, but by Longstreet's advice I never formally assumed command until after he left, which was not until after Gettysburg. We always divided the command without having any difficulty or disagreement. However, my attention was only recently called to an error which arose from this. On the second day's fight at Gettysburg, Henry was the more immediately in command, though we were both on the field. But on the third day Henry stayed on the right of our line. On that day I had part of the battalion immediately opposite the Cemetery Ridge, with some guns added to them. Henry was never there, and had no part in the battle for Cemetery Heights.[21]

One of the men who was with me has written, urging me to correct the monument which says that he was in command there, whereas he never went to the spot. I declined, as the poor fellow had a pitiful life. He had a sad end and is welcome to all the credit he can get. Besides, he was absent only because his duty was elsewhere. He was as brave a man as ever lived. We were good friends, and I would have been willing to do much more for him at a much greater sacrifice, if it had ever been in my power.

The day after I reached Culpeper and took command (Henry being absent) firing broke out early in the morning toward Stevensburg, an insignificant little settlement on our extreme right of the line in the famous battle of Brandy Station.[22] In the fighting the enemy tried to develop our position and troops, while our men attempted to mask the position and movements of our army. It was long and severe, and ended with the final repulse of the enemy, but with very heavy loss to our troops.

I was early ordered to move three batteries down the Stevensburg Road to a point about a mile short of where the fighting was. Soon stragglers from various regiments, chiefly from the 4th Virginia, began to pass. All told stories of disaster, putting much blame on the South Carolina cavalry, who were engaged lower down the road. One of these men told me that Colonel Butler [23] and Lieutenant Colonel Frank Hampton [24] had both been mortally wounded. I rode forward to investigate, as I had been very intimate at Colonel Hampton's house while at college, and like all who knew him, I was much attached to him.

I found that he was lying mortally wounded at a house near the road, while Butler had lost his leg and had been carried off to a hospital. The men who had been with Hampton said that the 4th Virginia had broken, and he had been shot while trying to make his men hold both their line and that of the 4th Virginia. Butler, who was commanding the whole brigade line, was struck by a shell which crushed his leg. I stayed with Colonel Hampton until his death and never heard a complaint from him.

A few days after this battle we started into Pennsylvania. Our army had daily orders to do no damage, and no troops could have passed through the country of their best friends with less harm. I heard of but one act of violence, the murder and robbery of an old man, and the first news we got of it was the sight of the two murderers, hanging by the roadside, having been executed by General Lee's orders.

We passed through Chambersburg and halted at a little settlement called Snickersville, just at the foot of the mountains. On the evening of the first of July we heard firing just across the mountain and were ordered in that direction. We marched all night, reaching the plain of Gettysburg about daybreak. As we got near we began to hear of the fight of the evening before and to see the wounded.

Here I visited the field hospital of Pettigrew's Brigade, which I had last seen in North Carolina. Major Iredell [25] of that brigade asked that I be called to tell him goodby, as he was dying. When I went to him, I was surrounded by men I had been thrown with in full health and spirits. I heard that Burgwyn, Marshall, Hughes, McCreary,[26] and many others who were my friends were dead on the field.

From there we marched only a short distance and halted to rest and feed just on the Emmitsburg Pike near where we opened the fight later that same day. We lay there until about four o'clock, when we were ordered to take a position not more than a hundred yards from where we had been since early morning and to open on the mountain opposite (Little Round Top).

Sometime earlier I, with several couriers and one of our officers, had ridden over the top of Round Top, finding only an enemy picket of two or three men, one of whom we captured. No body of the enemy was then in sight, but when we started in at four, stopping to tear a stone wall out of the way, a battery on the mountain, which had apparently just come up, opened on us with very fatal effect.[27]

As soon as we got into action, we silenced their battery quite easily. The top of the mountain seemed to be almost all rock, and when our shells struck they shattered and dashed the rock so as to be the equal of canister at short range. While this was going on Hood's Division was steadily climbing the side of the mountain under a sharp fire, reaching the top, but being almost immediately driven back by reinforcements, which the enemy rushed forward. Three times the top was taken, to be almost immediately lost. Hood's left meantime gained the lower ridges, capturing many prisoners and several guns, but his left flank was as regularly driven back by Sickles'[28] Division, stationed in the Peach Orchard on the road—the Emmitsburg Pike—into Gettysburg.

After the fight had gone on for about two hours, I was ordered to take two batteries to Hood. When I reported he turned, apparently to give me orders but at that instant he was struck on the arm by a shrapnel shot, reeled and fell from his horse, utterly prostrated and almost fainting. The wound, which was not very severe, seemed to shock him much more than a far more serious one would ordinarily have done. He was not a sensitive or nervous man, and members of his staff have told me that when his leg was crushed to fragments at Chickamauga,[29] he never lost his composure for a moment, and gave orders clearly and coolly before allowing himself to be taken from the field. He seemed to realize at Gettysburg that he could do nothing, and called out for General Law [30] and Dr. Darby. Law was his second in command, but as always in a fight was far in front with his foremost man. Before he could be found and came to take command, the battle was practically over and it was getting dark.

We went in and brought out the batteries the infantry had taken, but nothing more could be done until the next morning, when I was ordered to take two batteries down the road, and was placed by Colonel E. P. Alexander,[31] chief of artillery of Longstreet's Corps, in the Peach Orchard, where we engaged the enemy's batteries on Cemetery Heights. Some guns were farther to the right, but not on the line in front of Cemetery Ridge, and I had some other batteries under my direction, but only the two of my own.

We opened fire and so commenced the great artillery duel which began what has been called the pivotal attack of the war. For several hours the guns never ceased their fire and many were killed and wounded. At last the enemy's guns almost stopped firing, and we hoped—vainly as it turned out —that we had silenced them. Just about this time Colonel Alexander showed me a note he had received from Longstreet, telling him that when the time came—it meant when Alexander thought the full work of the artillery had been accomplished—to tell Pickett to charge.

Alexander very naturally hesitated to take such a responsibility, and answered Longstreet saying so. Longstreet immediately came up, and talked the matter over with Alexander, who said that he thought he had accomplished about all our guns could and besides, we were almost out of ammunition. Longstreet finally concluded that there was nothing more to wait for and sent the order to Pickett. At the same time he said, "It is all wrong, but he will have it," or words to that effect, referring to General Lee's decision to charge the enemy on Cemetery Heights.[32]

At the same time I was ordered to move with all the guns I could take from the line—I think only five—on Pickett's right flank. Having no special orders beyond that I was to help where I could, I moved about halfway to the heights. At that point I saw to our right, about five hundred yards away, possibly a little more, an immense body of the enemy's infantry, apparently deploying to take Pickett in the flank. I at once came into action and opened fire on them. Evidently the fire troubled them, for they drew back in considerable confusion, and a large number of guns—General Hunt,[33] who was their chief of artillery, told me after the war that there were six or eight batteries—opened on my guns at short range with most disastrous effect, killing and wounding a number of the men and dismounting two of the guns.

My ammunition gave out entirely about this time, and I sent out the men able to go, carrying such of the wounded who could move with their help. Then I ordered litters for the wounded who were too badly hurt to get out with only the assistance of their comrades, and had two of the company commanders bring in limber chests and ropes to take out the disabled guns. Soon all were out, but while waiting I was struck in the side by a heavy piece of shell. It was half-spent and striking my swordhilt did not go into my body, but knocked me from my horse. For a time it disabled me so that I was assisted to a large barn which was just on the left of my guns during the duel of the morning.[34]

When I got there I found General Pickett and his staff, his division by this time having got back, except for those who were killed or captured, in great confusion. I have had the statement very severely questioned by General Pickett's admirers as reflecting on him and denying him the credit which history has generally given him. But I repeat it positively and solemnly as a fact, which justice to the brave men that he commanded but did not lead demands.

If any proof is needed, look at the reports. While not a single general and scarcely a field officer came out of the charge unhurt, neither Pickett nor any of his staff—and he had a large and gallant one—was touched. I left him at the barn when I went in, and I found him at the barn—unscathed, when near all of the officers outside of him and his staff were killed and wounded—when I came out. Is it not reasonable to say that he was there all the time, and not leading the charge of his division as his admirers assert? It is most unpleasant to deny the claim of a soldier, but I think it a duty as holy as it is painful to do what one can that credit is not withheld or wrongly given.[35]

After the defeat of Pickett's men the two armies lay in front of each other until dark, and then we drew back. The next night we started to the Potomac and lay there waiting, but Meade [36] made no move and we fell back across the river. Here my friend General Pettigrew met his death. He was in command of Heth's Division after Heth [37] had been wounded the first day of the battle. He was with the rear guard, just above the ford at Williamsport, when a small body of the enemy's cavalry, crazed with whiskey, dashed in. Though they were all killed at once, one of them shot Pettigrew through the body, and he died after much suffering a few days later.[38]

Pettigrew seemed to have every attribute of a great soldier, uniting with the brightest mind and an active body a disposition which made him the idol of his men and a courage which nothing could daunt. He was so full of theoretical knowledge that I think it really impaired his usefulness, but experience, which he was getting fast, would have corrected that, and I believe that few would have had a brighter career.

In this battle (Gettysburg) my brother William was killed while commanding the skirmishers of Pender's [39] Division. He never rose above the rank of captain, though General A. P. Hill had just got General Lee's approval to form a regiment of skirmishers of which William was to be the colonel. He already had application from five times as many men as he could have taken.

He was a remarkable man. At college he made no great

success, barely getting his degree though a faithful student; yet many years after the war several of his old professors of the University of Virginia said to me that they expected more of him than of any student who attended the institution for many years. Fellow students, like Bishop Dudley of Kentucky and others distinguished in their lives, have told me how he was the most admired man in the University.

William was as deeply and simply religious as any man ever was, never obtruding it on anyone out of place, but never failing to assert it in the right place. More than one clergyman has told me how William's life in the army had converted him and made him devote his life to the church. Hundreds of his fellow soldiers have delighted to bear testimony to his bravery and devotion. As one said, "He was brave as only one who, at peace with his God, seemed utterly regardless of anything man could do." [40]

Once soon after the war, while riding through the mountains of North Carolina, I stopped to have my horse shod by an old blacksmith. We had often employed him while hunting in the mountains before the war, and he asked many questions about my brothers, especially William. He asked the details of his death and if he was leading his men. I could not answer his questions, and told him I had been miles away on another part of the field. The smith's striker, who was his son, had been with my brother, so the old man asked him. He said: "No, I can't say where he was. We never bothered to know where he was. We always knew he was in the right place to do us the most good, and if we could not see him we knew he was where he ought to be. If he was a half mile behind, every man knew he was there because there he could do the most good, and we knew that if he could do the most good by going right into the Yankees he would go right in. So we never bothered ourselves to know what he was doing." That seemed to be the reputation he had with all.

A few days after the battle of Gettysburg, my brother

Charles, who had been sent to command the extreme end of Morris Island in Charleston Harbor, was killed resisting the enemy's landing. On the same day my uncle, Langdon Cheves, who had volunteered, had been put on duty as an engineer, and had built Battery Wagner, the principal fort on Morris Island, was killed by almost the first shell thrown into it. My father and mother, who had gone to the county seat for news, got a letter, which told them of the three deaths.

The battle of Gettysburg will, no doubt, rank as the turning point of the war though perhaps it may better be called the breaking-point of the South's resources. For months our men had been on rations such as no troops ever campaigned on and did a tithe of the work ours were called on to do. Corn meal and damaged bacon were the staples, often so damaged that to live on them insured disease. Medicines, chloroform especially, had got so scarce that small operations as painful as great ones were done without it. Much of that which was used was of such bad quality that it was used as only a choice of evils.

Delicacies for the sick were unheard of. They lived on damaged bacon or lean beef or went hungry. Clothes and shoes were scant and insufficient, except for those which were taken from our friends, the enemy. Overcoats would have been almost unknown but for them, though for that matter we would have fared badly for everything but for their contributions.[41] Certainly half of our muskets and two-thirds of our artillery were forced contributions from them, while Banks,[42] who commanded the United States troops in the Valley in 1862, was better known as and better deserved the title of Jackson's commissary than as the commander of his troops.

This state of affairs would appear to give compelling reasons for the much criticized advance into Pennsylvania. With our railroad lines worn out, our ports blockaded, and the field of operations stripped by both armies, and burned and deso-

lated by the enemy, who at last openly declared that their
policy would be, as Sheridan [43] later boasted, to leave the
country so that a crow flying over it would have to carry his
rations,[44] the capture of arms, clothing, medicine, and even
food, which earlier had added to our comfort, now came to
be a necessity. It looked easier to go to the enemy's homes
to get it, and to leave our poor people a chance to rest and
to gather together the fragments left them.

Certainly, General Lee and President Davis must have appreciated the fearful odds that would meet us and the desperate chances we would take. Yet who can say that they were
not wise to risk all, and not to sit down, to be worn out by
armies successively defeated but always renewed and sent
back, to wear out by attrition those whom they could not
defeat in open fight. As to the conduct of the advance and
whether victory was possible, critics will always differ. I
feel that to criticize is possibly presumptuous yet it is well
for each who has opinions to express them. I do so, not feeling
very much confidence in them or any pride of opinions; but
hope that where my opinions are unfavorable as to the course
of our leaders, the better judgment of wiser men will hold
that I am wrong.

I think we were weighted by first, a demoralized army, and
for this I hold General Lee largely responsible. He had an
apparent antipathy to anything partaking of pomposity and
the vanity of war, but he had an utterly undue regard for the
value of the elementary teaching of West Point and for the
experience gained by the very small police duty of our minia-
ture regular army. He failed to realize that while a military
school is excellent for the training of drill masters, who are
most necessary, it teaches little of military science in comparison with the hard experience of a single campaign. When an
army is confined for military leaders to a handful of lieutenants, who have never seen more than a regiment, probably
not more than a company, in action, and have never had to

deal with a harder problem in the maintenance of their men than how to get a wagon train from the nearest railroad station, it is apt to be hurt by the restriction. And it was often difficult to get past the incompetents, who went in as drill masters and were then pushed up by the ability of their men, who were of a class few armies have ever seen, to become commanders of large operations.[45]

Such a leader as Napoleon could and did see the greatest cavalry leader of the age in the stable boy, Murat, and found such great lieutenants as Ney, Junot, Lannes, Bessières, Massena, and a host of others among those whose only learning came to them in the experience of the campaign and the lessons of numerous battles. But General Lee never went outside, and was apparently resolute against doing so, the regular grades to find officers, who might have been very Samsons to help him multiply his scant resources. He never discovered or encouraged a Forrest, and many a man went to his death, trying to win against the incompetency of leaders who should have been brushed out of the way when they failed.

When the fall of the year came, and General Lee sent his list to fill vacancies, they came out in alphabetical order. The dodger, who lived while another died, trying to do his own and another's duty, got rank, and the hero got an unmarked grave. I have heard in these latter days of more than one who said that he was promoted on the field of battle. But no one heard of such a thing in the war; in fact, there was no authority vested in anyone to promote except with a full measure of red tape and routine.[46] Perhaps the nearest case of promotion on the field was that of J. B. Gordon,[47] who at the Wilderness,[48] breaking through the enemy's line with a brigade, saved his flanks by wheeling one half of his brigade to the right and the other to the left, sweeping both ways. His promotion was asked by wire and promptly sent, but if I am not mistaken, it was made because the rank was necessary to enable him to take command where he was needed.[49]

The man in our army who first made this move was Colonel Abner Perrin.[50] He dashed through the Pennsylvania Bucktails [51] at Gettysburg, swinging his remnant of a brigade to right and left, and swept from the field an enemy command which had held our troops in check for hours with terrible losses. Yet he was not noticed until over two months after, when he did get a tardy promotion, along with many others who had risen strictly by reason of seniority to take the place of those who lost their lives because they took no pains to save them.[52] Nor was there anything to note any difference for Perrin from those, some of whom, at least, had they fought as he did, would have died, as Perrin did but a little after.

A further, crushing weight was that we had among our division commanders more than one or two, who were far inferior to a number of their regimental officers. And not only did the incompetency of these generals hold back their commands, but the men and officers, both of whom by this time appreciated the true value of their commanders, were getting tired of sacrificing themselves under leaders who did them no credit and whom they distrusted. It is very near the literal truth that an army of sheep, led by a lion, will defeat an army of lions with a sheep for a commander. We had too many sheep commanders.

Again, at Gettysburg, there is no doubt but that we suffered for lack of information. Our cavalry did not give us the timely information, or the time to get ready, which was their chief duty. If Stuart, instead of being miles away, had been in position guarding our advance, giving our infantry warning, engaging the enemy and masking our troops until they all got together, there is every reason to think that we might have crushed the enemy in detail. As it was, our Second and Third Corps blundered into them, and without knowing their numbers or positions fought and defeated them the first day. Then, ignorant of the country and of the forces before them, the two corps drew back to wait for the rest of the army, giving up voluntarily positions which General Lee spent his army trying to get back in the next two days. Whose fault this was, I cannot say, but Napoleon would not have let it occur.

Longstreet has been blamed greatly for the delay on the second and third days, I can't say how justly. But I well remember that on the second day we—the First Corps, which Longstreet commanded—got on the field by dawn and lay there until four o'clock before we were ordered to attack. About noon I remember that Lee and Longstreet rode up together and sat for half an hour on the very spot where my guns opened the fight at 4 P.M. At that time the infantry was in a quarter of a mile of the position where they began fighting that afternoon, and I have never understood why, if General Lee wanted the fight to begin, what delayed it then. Surely he could have begun it, had he so desired.[53]

I know further that after they left, I rode with a few mounted men all over both Round Tops, and the only Yankees we saw were a few pickets on top of Little Round Top. There Hood's Division was almost destroyed, trying to capture the position we could have occupied without a shot two hours earlier; one which, looking down on the rear of Cemetery Heights, would have rendered utterly untenable the position which, next day, we spent our whole strength trying to take. From the first to the last at Gettysburg, each move was made just an hour or so too late. This is the story of the battle as I saw it, perhaps wrongly as far as my conclusions go, but truthfully as I tell it. There are probably many good reasons for the things that look inexplicable. I only give such facts as I saw.

Returning to the matter of the neglect of special gallantry, I recall two additional cases. At Spotsylvania, some of my guns were occupying some half-finished works, and were carrying on quite an active duel with the enemy's artillery.

From a slight elevation I could see the smoke of their guns, when they fired, in time to signal my men to get under cover. One time a private—before he was a soldier, he was a fisherman on the North Carolina coast—dropped at the signal behind an unfinished breastwork, putting his face against it. The shot hit immediately in front and coming through, struck fair in his face with force enough to crush it. Then the shot rolled to the gun. In a moment he was up, and insisted on loading the shot in one of our guns and firing it back.

The other incident was again about a private, whose name I am ashamed to say I forget. He was sitting with his comrades in a gun-pit, where a quantity of fused ammunition with some loose straw thrown carelessly on it lay around them. The straw caught fire from a bursting enemy shell. Cartridges and shells began to explode, and it looked as though all might be killed, when the man whose name I don't remember quickly picked up shell after shell, some of them with their fuses burning, and dropped one after the other into a small mud-puddle nearby. When practically all were in, one of them burst in his hands, but wonderful to say only taking two of his fingers.

I made special reports of both cases, and both were granted sick leave, but without a word of commendation. Going home, they found their cabins and their families as they had left them, with fish a-plenty and a better market—the United States soldiers—than they had known. They took the oath of allegiance and stayed at home. Their families needed them. There was no glory for them, no cross of a legion of honor. Their duty to a cause they scarce understood, hardship, suffering, and danger of death were all they had to return to. The danger and suffering to them and their families were great, their reward invisible. Who can wonder that they stayed home or judge them harshly? I for one cannot. The true wonder is that any held out. Many a morning in camp I have read appeal after appeal for leave to go home from good men, who would attach to their petitions letters from their wives, with appeals for the men to come home to save their families from starvation and cold. The pity of it, when we remember those whose hearts failed and were taken, to be made sad examples of, becomes almost too much.[54]

Chapter 5

Tangle in the Wilderness

AFTER the return of our army to the south side of the Potomac, we slowly fell back from point to point till we took up lines south of the Potomac. For a long time there was little fighting. My immediate command made its winter quarters, first near Gordonsville and finally at Lindsay and Cobham stations on the railroad from Gordonsville to Charlottesville, Longstreet's infantry went to the assistance of Bragg and the Army of Tennessee, and Alexander's artillery accompanied it.[1] The rest of the artillery remained with General Lee's force. Longstreet ordered me to go with him, and I started but was ordered back.

During the winter we had several engagements, the most important being Bristoe's Station,[2] on the railroad five or six miles south of Manassas Junction. There we were roughly handled and repulsed by the enemy under Warren. We struck them and drove them back at first, with a small loss of prisoners by them and killed and wounded on both sides, until Warren formed a line on the opposite side of the railroad from his wagons, with some artillery crowded in the angle of quite a deep creek and the railroad and a skirmish line some distance away on a small ridge. Our men, seeing only the

61

skirmish line on the hill above them, rushed down to catch it before it could be moved off. As they got within a very short distance, Warren's line of battle, in front of his skirmish line and in the railroad cut, rose and poured in a deadly fire, which entirely broke and repulsed our advance, inflicting great loss. Before the disaster could be remedied, the enemy got across the creek and well toward their fortifications at Manassas Junction. General Heth commanded the division which attacked at this point, and two of his brigade commanders, Generals John R. Cooke [3] and W. W. Kirkland,[4] were severely wounded.

Bristoe Station was a most unfortunate blunder, as it cost us a good many men and we lost large stores which would have been most valuable to us. It could have been easily avoided too, as a section of artillery up the railroad, where we had full possession of it, would have so completely enfiladed the enemy's position as to make it utterly untenable. I never heard who was responsible for it. General Lee was present, but he never took the army into his confidence, less than ever after a disaster.[5]

Later we were all marched out in great haste in a terrible spell of cold weather to meet Meade at Mine Run.[6] It was the coldest period we ever undertook to campaign in, but Meade's heart apparently failed him and after a day of very sharp skirmishing we lay for two more in the cold, a number of men freezing and more being killed later by pneumonia, only to find out, at last, that Meade had given up his threatening advance and had stolen away in the night.

General Lee has been blamed for letting Meade get away without more punishment, but I know no more of the merits than the bulk of the army or the critics, and incline to think that General Lee saw the situation clearer than any of them.

All the rest of the period until spring we spent in winter quarters near Green Spring Valley,[7] where we were most hospitably entertained by the citizens, who up to this time had suffered comparatively little from the enemy. About the middle of April Longstreet brought his corps back from Tennessee, and my battalion, along with the rest of his artillery which had remained behind in Virginia, joined him, and very soon after we marched to the Wilderness where the series of battles with Grant began.

On the fifth of May we heard the firing of the first day at the Wilderness [8] and pressed forward all night. About daylight we were double-quicked for about two miles and got to the plank road from Fredericksburg to Orange soon after it got light. All of Longstreet's artillery was absent except my battalion, the rest having been left some distance back. I was with Longstreet most of the 6th, but even my guns, which were there for service, did nothing to amount to anything. It was more exclusively a small arms fight than any battle of the war.

When Longstreet, at the head of his corps, reached the road, the men of Hill's Corps, who had been rushed by the enemy while they were still in their bivouacs, were breaking through the lines Longstreet was trying to form and crying out that the enemy was on them in enormous force. In fact, they were utterly panic-stricken, and for a time it looked as if there was bound to be a headlong stampede. But Longstreet, always grand in battle, never shone as he did here. Riding to the front, he shouted his commands and made the men hear them, telling Kershaw, commanding the first division and a most superb soldier, to form his line with picked officers as guides and color bearers. Longstreet rode up and down the lines, encouraging, exhorting, and steadying the men, with an effect on them that no other leader I ever saw had on his troops. In a short time he had the line straightened out and steadied, with the men pouring volley after volley into the enemy, who were only a short distance away.

But the enemy continued to press steadily forward and kept up a most terrific fire into our men. Often the two lines were not more than a hundred yards apart. The ground was thickly covered with scrub oak saplings, and there was scarcely one to be found at the end of the day that was not scarred by shot. All that a horseman could do was to try to keep his horse off the wounded men, without regard for the dead. It looked as if no human being could stand under such sheets of fire as were flashing back and forth.

Grant's men pushed forward, flushed with apparent success until they met Longstreet's men. The enemy could not give up what they thought was assured victory, and fought as we had never seen them fight. But Longstreet, the greatest fighter and tactician our war produced, and his troops, whom Hooker [9] once called the finest infantry the world ever saw, were not to be stopped. After such a stubborn struggle as war has hardly ever seen, the Union troops began to give back, slowly at first, then faster, and finally they left the field routed.

When they started to give way, Longstreet ordered me to bring up a battery, which I did. Putting two guns on the plank road, we advanced some distance, raking the woods on either side, but it effected little and was soon stopped. While we were advancing I noticed a large, fine-looking man in the uniform of a general, who was lying on the side of the road in the dust and heat. Noticing that he was still alive, I had two of my orderlies to move him out of the dust. They stuck some muskets up and spread a blanket over him as an awning, then got a surgeon to examine him. The surgeon did not think that he was conscious, and gave him some water and morphine. He had been shot through the head and died not very long afterwards. He was General Wadsworth [10] of New York, and was said by some of the prisoners who knew him to have been a very brave man.

After this desperate fight there was a pause for some time to rest the men, to get the lines straightened, and to replenish ammunition. Then Longstreet, after a long conference with General Lee,[11] and with General Jenkins,[12] of South Carolina and General Mahone,[13] of Virgina, moved on. Soon the men of our corps were sharply engaged. They drove the enemy slowly but steadily until finally the Union troops were routed. Then our men halted to wait for Mahone, who, it appeared, was obliquing to the same spot that Jenkins was aiming for. In a few minutes we could see Mahone's men coming rapidly to the meeting-point, having routed the enemy in their front.

Longstreet rode near to Jenkins' column. Jenkins was jubilant. He had thoroughly done his work in most brilliant style and knew that his promotion to major general was assured. He rode out to meet Longstreet and called to the men to cheer him, which they did with a will. Jenkins' Brigade was one of those which had recently returned from the South, and the men were dressed in new uniforms made of cloth so dark a gray as to be almost black. Mahone's men, some distance off in the thick underbrush, hearing the cheers and seeing this body of dark uniformed men, took them for Yankees and fired a volley. Fortunately they fired high, or there would have been a terrible slaughter. As it was, while they only struck eight or ten mounted men, the effect was horrible, for among the few were Jenkins, shot through the head, and Longstreet, through the neck.

Both fell, Jenkins instantly, Longstreet—whose nerve nothing ever shook—first moving forward and waving his left hand (his right arm was paralyzed by the shot) to Mahone's troops, who recognized him and stopped, horror-stricken at what they had done. Longstreet was hardly on the ground when he beckoned members of the staff, and pulling their heads to his lips, for he could only whisper, sent them to find General Lee and to tell him that the enemy were in utter rout, and if pressed, would all be his before night.

I was one of those whom Longstreet sent, but Colonel Latrobe [14] of Baltimore, Longstreet's inspector general, was the first to find General Lee and to give him Longstreet's message. General Lee at once rode to the point and sent for

General R. H. Anderson, who had been my first chief on Sullivan's Island, to take command of the corps. All this took time, the enemy recovered from their panic and were offering some resistance when our men moved forward in a feeble-hearted way. The chance which we had never had before and were never to have again was lost.[15]

The wounding of Longstreet and Jenkins was even more disastrous than the death of Jackson. Jackson had to a large extent accomplished his object, and left his force in a position so that Stuart could and did complete the victory. Longstreet fell just as his move had utterly routed and demoralized the enemy, while the fall of Jenkins, who was the life of the move and might have finished it, for he feared no danger and no responsibility, at the same time left no one to carry it on.[16]

I was with Jenkins for an hour later in the day. He never, though unconscious until he was almost gone, forgot the fight. He would cheer his men and implore them to sweep the enemy into the river, until he became too weak to talk. He was a remarkable man, full of spirit and enthusiasm, and as full of the most resolute courage. He could lead a charge as dashingly as Murat and repel one as stubbornly as Ney. We lost him, like many another good man, because he thought when he fought only where he could go to do the enemy the most harm, never of himself. He was my brother Charles' classmate at military school, and spent his last Christmas before graduation at our home in Abbeville, where he was a favorite of the entire household.

After the terrible thrashing we had given the enemy our only thought and regret was that, as usual, the Yankees would get back over the river, refit, and come at us again after a long time of rest. But we found to our cost that in Grant we had a different quality of opponent with whom to deal: that killing and disabling one army only brought a fresh one against our tired and half-fed men, for Grant, having reasoned his problem as being one of wearing out our tens of thousands with his hundreds of thousands, would never hesitate. In twenty-four hours we were going as hard as we could to prevent him from getting between us and Richmond, and barely succeeded in getting ahead of him at Spotsylvania.[17]

After the Battle of the Wilderness, I was ordered to fall in the rear, to rest and pasture my horses. But on the morning of the 8th, while we halted on the side of the road to let the troops pass by, to get where we could hear firing beyond, young Pegram, of Baltimore, a courier of Stuart, came riding rapidly. He showed me an open dispatch from Stuart to either Lee or Longstreet, asking for artillery to be sent to him as he was hard pressed. Endorsing on it that I had gone, I went as fast as I could. About a mile from Spotsylvania I met Stuart, who had formed his men so as to protect the road, and was urging on infantry to hold the line in the face of the heavy forces which were being thrown against him.

Stuart took me down to the Block House,[18] where the roads crossed, and placed my guns on a low range of hills, where we were very soon hotly engaged. He was obliged to move most of his men to the right, to meet the constantly extending line of the enemy, and left me only a line of skirmishers. As soon as Stuart went to the right, they went to their regiments, so I was left fighting infantry and artillery, without any protection. But by placing my batteries in echelon and far apart, I was able to protect one partially by the crossfire of another.

The main point of the enemy attack was on Potts' North Carolina Battery, and the fight was such as I never saw before. At one time the guns of the battery were firing in three different directions at infantry which was advancing to take them. The mortality was terrific, and when the company was relieved by the arrival of our infantry, over half the men were dead or wounded. There was no ammunition left except for a few rounds of solid shot. Strange as it may seem, this was much more efficacious for breaking a charging line than shrapnel and canister, which while disabling twice as many did not make such a crashing noise.

Among our dead was Captain Potts,[19] who had taken the company when badly demoralized and had brought it to so fine a standard that even when subjected to such a fire as artillery was seldom called on to stand, there was never a moment's pause in the continuity of firing. It was kept up even when the guns were worked by the officers and orderlies as cannoneers.

The next morning Stuart rode some distance out of his way to see me and to ask after Potts, who had died in the night. When I told him that the company was utterly disabled by its casualties and that the others had suffered heavily, he wrote and sent to General Lee a request that incoming recruits should be sent to the battalion until it was filled up. At the same time he paid it a high compliment, and asked me to let him apply for me to be sent to him. Then we parted, with him going to meet the enemy and his death three days later at Yellow Tavern.[20]

I was ordered to fall back to the reserve line to refit and numbers of recruits were sent to me, and I took no further part in the Spotsylvania fight until the day of the Bloody Angle.[21] On that day the musketry fire never ceased its roar for over sixteen hours. At one point a tree over a foot in diameter was cut down by musket balls (a section of it is now in a government building in Washington). In the fight Major Watson [22] of the Second Corps artillery, who highly distinguished himself, was killed, and his artillery being partly disabled I was ordered to move in two batteries. As I marched in, there was a close rank of wounded and dying coming out. In less than two hundred yards I met two wounded brigadiers and one, an old North Carolina friend, General Daniel, who had been killed.[23] I was stopped before I got in, as the enemy had been checked, so that, while I was on duty, I was not actually engaged in the battle.

Here, we thought that Grant would certainly have had enough for the season, but shortly we again found ourselves making a forced march to cut him off at Cold Harbor, where we formed our lines and had some terrible fighting.[24] It was at Cold Harbor that Grant earned his title of "Butcher," and deserved it. He hurled his troops time after time against our men in earthworks from which he could not have driven them with the whole Yankee nation to back him. How many men he sacrificed will, I suppose, never be told, but the ground in front of our works was covered black with the dead, besides the thousands who were carried off or made their way back, wounded. He never stopped till his men, themselves, refused to be longer uselessly slaughtered.

While in these lines a circumstance occurred which showed a remarkable side of the soldiers' character. One evening I was ordered by General Lee to fire on a piece of woods in front of us, and on doing so I stirred up a perfect hornets' nest. It appeared that in some way General Lee, who personally gave me the order, had found that the enemy were moving to the left through this body of woods. As soon as I opened fire a number of guns were brought against me, with about as hot a fire as was ever seen. Our earthworks were good, so our loss was small, while that of the enemy was enormous, considering the number of our guns engaged. But the fire was so appalling that one of my batteries, about half a mile to my right, almost stopped, which made it much hotter for the others. The captain, a most gallant man, did not realize the importance of our fire being kept up. I had to start him up again.

I had my horse under a steep hill back of our position in what had been an old ice-house, dug in the side of the hill. Running down in a lull in the firing, I mounted and dashed to the battery. As I reached it a shot struck my horse, cutting his leg off just below the shoulder and throwing me violently off him. I was carried in, soon got all right, and put the guns to work. My poor horse, in the meantime, had gone stumbling down the hill. He was the fastest horse in the corps, and in the favorite amusement of saddle-horse races was never beaten. My men were always ready to stake their all on him. As none of them would do it, after the fight I got a man of another regiment to go and shoot him. When it was done, the men set to work and dug a deep grave, so that the buzzards could not get him. They buried him in it and put a headboard over him, though there were any number of dead men left on the ground. Thus the horse fared better than the men.

After the fighting at Cold Harbor died down, some of our men got so close to the works as to find the enemy had evacuated them, so from here we moved to Malvern Hill,[25] where two years before McClellan had repulsed us and escaped to his boats. There was not much fighting here. At the end of two days, in changing some of our troops they got close to the earthworks of the enemy, who had got clear away from us. We did not get to them until Beauregard had repulsed them at Bermuda Hundred[26] and was fighting hard to keep them out of Petersburg,[27] which he succeeded in doing until we got there to his support.

Chapter 6

In Front of Petersburg

AT Petersburg both armies fortified their lines and lay opposite each other until the following spring. We did a great deal
of fighting, gradually wearing out our half-fed, half-clothed
men. When we got there, we were just in time to keep Grant's
troops out. They had broken our line in more than one place,
and we only drove them back far enough to form our line
connectedly, although with many angles and salients in it,
something which would never have been, if we had had the
opportunity to select it before the fighting began.

Our line at the point where I was located—immediately
in front of Petersburg—was about a mile from the thickly
settled part of the town, while the enemy's works were not
more than a half mile from ours. The advance lines and
rifle-pits were much closer to each other. In fact, at the
point where the battle of the Crater was fought, their rifle-
pits were not more than one hundred and fifty yards from our
main line. This made the position terribly trying to our men,
who could never be off their guard. They could not expose
themselves without being instantly fired on at short range by
the enemy. Moreover the enemy frequently relieved the men
in their advance line, while ours were on constant duty.

The Jerusalem Plank Road ran about three hundred yards back of our main line, on the crest of a ridge running in front of Petersburg. Between this ridge and the town there was a ravine, which ran parallel to the ridge and was about a hundred feet deep with a stream at the bottom. This stream flowed into the Appomattox River, which ran around the north side of the town.

The dust and the heat were appalling, as the line ran along a red clay ridge without a tree near. But if the men ever for a moment stood up straight or left the line only a few feet, unless they went out by ditches, and even then it was dangerous, they exposed themselves to almost certain death. The soldiers finally raised the earthworks a foot above their heads, and constructed from the ravine a covered way, which ran across the plank road to our lines, and provided a reasonably safe means of approach to our lines. But this constant need for precaution going on for months was terribly wearing on our troops.

I kept part of my command on the front line, with the rest of it in reserve in the deep ravine I have described. Sometime in July I received orders from Corps Headquarters to keep two batteries harnessed with the men sleeping by the guns. For some days orders were given to be specially prepared, but about the third night of these special orders, I was in my tent, sleeping with my clothes on and my horse standing saddled by the tent, when just as day was breaking we were aroused by a terrible explosion which was followed by several others in quick succession.[1] As I ran out of my tent and gave orders to my orderly-bugler to sound the alarm, the whole sky was lighted by the explosions. From nearly a mile off we could see in the light of the flashes men being blown in the air. We at once dashed up the hill with the two batteries which were ready and took position on the plank road, immediately in front, occupying some half-completed gunpits and placing some guns in a shallow sink in the road, which made pretty effective protection.

The enemy, meantime, had poured into the Crater and the adjacent earthworks, which, perhaps for one or two hundred yards on each side of the Crater, had been abandoned by our men, who were panic-stricken by the terrible explosion which had roused them from their sleep and buried hundreds of their comrades. There was nothing to stop the enemy from going into Petersburg and cutting General Lee's army in two but their timidity and inefficiency and the failure of their officers. Even after I got my guns into position, a couple of good companies, deployed as skirmishers, could have taken them with little trouble; the ground was rough and broken, for protection, and the distance not over three hundred yards, but they did not attempt it. The papers told how they charged, crying no quarter, and were driven back by a storm of shot and shell at the very muzzles of the guns, but we who manned the guns saw nothing of this. Time after time, they did come part of the way, only to break as we threw a few shells into them, and the only cries we heard were appeals for quarter of a good many who saw the way shorter into our lines than back into theirs.

Still, we did not doubt that in a little while they would come in earnest, so I called for volunteers to stay, telling those who wished to leave to man some guns for which we had no room. None went, so I had a number of the spare men to pick up muskets, which the enemy had dropped as they ran in, and act as sharpshooters, to keep down a few of the enemy who were coming too close. Our men quickly rallied and were in high spirits. They made the prisoners who had charged into our lines go out and gather arms and ammunition under the fire from their friends. They bitterly protested, but I thought it no more than fair that, as they had come in, they should earn their own living, and did not stop it. But not very many were hurt.

We lay there, expecting every minute that someone among the enemy with brains and luck enough to come and take us would turn up, but they did not. While we were waiting I went down to where the regiments of Elliott's [2] Brigade were lying in a short ravine, which ran from the covered way toward the Crater and nearly up to it. There I found Elliott re-forming his men and disposing of them as well as he could, in preparation to resist the advance which all expected the enemy to make at any minute.

Elliott had recently come on from South Carolina, having been promoted to a brigadier general for his defense of Fort Sumter,[3] which will, if justice be done, rank beyond any defense of a besieged position in history. He entered the fort when it was but a heap of ruins, commanded on the one side by enormous enemy batteries on the adjacent islands and on the others by Federal war vessels. Although the best engineers reported it as untenable and advised that the garrison be withdrawn, he held it against attacks in apparently overwhelming force. With the help of his engineer officer, Captain Johnson—now the Reverend John Johnson, rector of St. Paul's Parish of Charleston—he replaced at night the sandbag protection, which the enemy fire had destroyed during the day. He never did give up, and finally the enemy abandoned the attack. He was then sent on to Virginia.

I told Elliott that I was almost helpless, if the enemy made the slightest effort, and that I was in pressing need of some sharpshooters to keep down those of the enemy who were making some demonstrations. He at once agreed with me, but told me that his men were very much demoralized and he doubted if he could do much to help. He ordered some of them to move, but they were slow doing it. While he walked in front of them and exhorted them, he was severely wounded and taken from the field.

We stood where we were until near mid-day, firing on the enemy from our position along the plank road and on either side of that part of our lines held by the enemy, but chiefly from a point on our right of the Crater, where two batteries commanded the approach to it from the enemy's lines. These batteries, which had recently joined the army from West Virginia, were at first utterly demoralized and for a time did nothing, but Major Gibbes [4] of South Carolina took command of them, with the aid of, first, my brother, Captain Joseph Haskell, assistant adjutant general of the First Corps artillery, and, later, Colonel Huger,[5] acting chief of artillery for the First Corps, rallied them, and made them do good work. They greatly interfered with the efforts of the enemy to send in fresh troops, and demoralized those already in, by keeping up a constant fire whenever any of them showed themselves. Gibbes was severely wounded, but had done the work before he was disabled.

A battery of my battalion, commanded by Captain Lamkin,[6] had some mortars on the plank road, and did some wonderful work in demoralizing and damaging the enemy at a distance of only a few hundred yards. The mortars quickly had the range with great accuracy, dropping shell after shell among the enemy and taking any fight they may have had in them out of them pretty thoroughly. Notwithstanding this comfortable state of affairs, those of us who had had experience could not imagine it possible that such a state of cowardly incompetency could last long among the enemy, and were trying to resign ourselves to seeing the war end for us right there, when suddenly we saw, coming up the covered way at double-quick, men who showed that they were veterans. To our immense relief we found it was Mahone's Division, and that he was with them. There was no better division and no better commander. Everything changed at once.

Mahone, with the cool promptness and dash which were peculiarly his own, at once made his arrangements. Sending for me, he questioned me as to the situation, and directed me to continue the artillery and mortar fire. He told me to advance some light mortars, which could be carried by the men to a point near the Crater, with the protection of his men, and with these to keep up a rapid fire. We got closer and closer to the enemy, until we were throwing shells with such light charges of powder that they would rise so slowly as to look as if they could not get to the enemy, who were so close that we could hear them cry out when the shells would fall among them, and repeatedly they would dash out and beg to surrender.

After some time at this, Mahone told me that he thought that the enemy were in a proper state of demoralization, and he ordered the charge, directing me to stop firing. Nevertheless the enemy made considerable resistance, and the fire was very severe. Mahone's Virginia Brigade, which moved against the Crater from our left, carried everything before it, but the one on our right, exposed to a terrible fire from the Crater obliqued to its left. This left part of our lost line and all the Crater still in the hands of the enemy, so a second charge was necessary.

Before making it, Mahone ordered me to see if I could not get closer to the enemy with my Eprouvette [7] mortars and demoralize them some more. I advanced the mortars all along the line, took two of them into the trenches we had recaptured. The enemy were again so close that we could hear them calling, so we began throwing shells with squibs for charges, and every few minutes numbers would dash into our lines crying for quarter.

Here I fired the first shot that I ever had personally in the war. I was walking forward in the trench to see ahead, with a view to advancing farther my mortars, when a lieutenant of Mahone's Division, seeing that I was not armed, handed me a pistol, and told me that I was liable at any corner to run against some of the enemy. Taking and cocking his pistol, I moved forward and at the very next turn, only a few steps beyond, ran square into a white man and two negroes. The white man called to the negroes to fire, and at the same time raised his pistol. I jumped back, firing at the white man as I did so, and called to our men to charge. They dashed around the corner and got fifteen or twenty negro soldiers, who were close behind the white man I had fired at. I found him lying on his face, shot through the head. He was, one of the negroes told me, the colonel of their regiment, but like all the officers of negro regiments, he had no insignia of rank. I never saw one of them with any in a fight; they had learned that our men did not readily give quarter to officers of negro regiments, so they preferred, when caught, to pass themselves as privates of white regiments.

Almost immediately after this incident, Mahone ordered his final charge, which took the entire line. I was still in the trench when the rush was made, and was carried, although without intending it, right into the Crater, which was packed full of Yankees, largely negroes. Our men, who were always made wild by having negroes sent against them, remembering that hundreds of their fellows were perhaps only then smothering under the piled-up dirt, were utterly frenzied with rage. Nothing in the war could have exceeded the horrors that followed. No quarter was given, and for what seemed a long time, fearful butchery was carried on. There was little firing, the men being too crowded together, but they stabbed with their bayonets and clubbed with their muskets until utterly exhausted, with fresh men coming in at every moment. Some of the white men were spared but very few negroes.

Taking no part, I was yet so covered with blood that I threw away my coat to get rid of the horror of its being soaked through. A favorite orderly was with me. A very powerful and plucky fellow, he had on my belt with a pistol in the holster, while I carried only a light fencing-sword in my hand. Suddenly I threw it up, almost involuntarily, to ward off a most unexpected bayonet thrust from a negro, who—like a cornered rat—had thrust at me. I drove at him but only touched him as he fell. As I stepped forward to strike him, he threw up his hands and in true, "rice-field Gullah" begged his life, which I had no desire to take.

Goodwyn, my orderly, at once stepped forward to shoot him, but I stopped him. I told the negro to go to the rear, which he most decidedly declined to do, as he expressed perfect confidence that if he ever left me he would be killed by "some white gentleman." I kept him with me and later sent him to help in the hospital where the wounded Yankees were, and never saw him again. To the last he begged that I should send him home to the cotton fields, where he would be a faithful worker. He, like all the rest of them, swore that he was taken into the Yankee army against his will.

Shortly after this I heard a fearful cry for protection; looking around I saw my orderly about to shoot a rather good-looking Yankee, and stopped him. He told me that this man had caught up a musket, and shouting out that he would kill the "damned niggers," had dashed out the brains of a colored soldier. My negro prisoner was by me still; on my asking him he said that the man was his captain and that the dead negro was also a member of the company. I heard of more than one other case, but this I saw. I told the man that I thought he well deserved the death to which the orderly at once put him.

When all was over I started back to my quarters. When I got down into the ravine, of which I have spoken, I met a soldier (only a home guard, I think) walking back toward the front with a colored sergeant in front of him. Suspecting his intentions, I stopped him and asked him what he was going for. He answered that he was taking his prisoner out to shoot him, and refused to turn back when I ordered him to do so. What the result would have been is doubtful but some soldiers who knew me happened to come up just then. They quickly made him obey, and took him to the guardhouse and the negro to my camp. Next day, I sent him to the hospital where the wounded prisoners were.

Walking immediately behind the soldier and his prisoner when I met them was a negro boy of eighteen or twenty, whom I recognized as a servant of Stephen Elliott. I told him to come on, and I would see that he went back to his master at the hospital. As we walked along he kept up a constant grumbling. Finally I asked him what he was saying. He answered that I "ought to have let that white man kill that Yankee negro." Rather shocked, I asked why he wanted him killed. He frankly answered, so that he might get his clothes. I sent him back under guard to his master and never saw him again. He may have risen to political prominence under the beneficent reconstruction government with which our Yankee brethren blessed our country after the Union was restored.[8]

Next day, in going to the front, I found a lot of wounded negroes, about forty or fifty, lying by the branch that ran from the ravine. The poor wretches were utterly miserable, and begged for water, which the camp negroes and colored loafers, while making fun of their suffering, refused them. On asking, I found that they had been out there by orders of a Yankee surgeon, a prisoner, who had said that there was no place for them in the locust grove hospital, which had been assigned to the wounded prisoners.

My orderlies gave them water, and I went back to camp, where I called up my body-servant, a very faithful fellow. I appealed to him to get the other camp servants, of whom he was an acknowledged leader, and to take these poor suffering wretches to the hospital.

He promptly refused, saying that, slave though he was, he would die first. On trying others, I found them all of the same way of thinking. I called on my assistant surgeon, named Nichols, a man to whom every man in the command was devoted, because of his care of them. He was a fine man, though rather a rough diamond, and he agreed to do something for the negroes. He soon got as many white men as he needed, loaded the prisoners in wagons on straw beds and hauled them to the hospital. He put them in with the white prisoners, gave them needed attention, and finally left them to the care of the Union doctors, on their promise to give the negroes proper attention. However, I heard later that they got so little care that all who were at all badly hurt died.

When Fort Harrison was taken by the enemy, I was ordered to the north side of the James River, as I have told before. There I was wounded in October and retired for several weeks, but I have already given an account of that fight and my experience.[9] In Petersburg, people were very kind and though in daily peril entertained as if no war was going on. I remember one night attending a ball at the house of Mr. W. R. Johnson.[10] This ball was attended, not only by the ladies of Petersburg, but by numbers of others who had come over from Richmond. While it was going on, two twelve-inch shells fell in the little front yard, bursting and throwing dirt over guests who were in the garden, but only stopping the dance for perhaps five minutes. People paid scarcely any attention to the shelling, though several non-combatants were killed by it. There was no justification for it, and it was done in sheer, brutal wantonness. The firing could hurt no one but women, children, and old men.

The day after I got back to the battalion, Grant made an attack on both of our flanks—on the Nine Mile Road and others running out of Richmond, and on the Petersburg. The heaviest fighting on the south side of the James was about Burgess's Mill,[11] where the principal fighting was by Hampton's cavalry. The enemy was defeated with heavy loss, but also inflicted heavy losses on our army.

General Hampton had two sons with him: Preston, his aide-de-camp, and Wade, who was an aide to General Joseph E. Johnston but was then visiting his father. Preston was killed while leading a charge, and Wade was severely wounded taking Preston out. Several others, of General Hampton's staff and couriers, were killed or wounded, among them his adjutant general, Major Theodore Barker.[12] The fight was very severe and bloody, but ended in a decided defeat for Hancock,[13] who commanded the enemy.

On the north side of the river, while the fighting was not nearly so severe, it was still quite heavy on the Darbytown and adjacent roads. Longstreet had returned from the absence caused by the wound he got at the Wilderness, and his presence was felt at once. He met and defeated the enemy's every advance over a line which was much too long for his men to occupy except in a thin skirmish order. But under his handling, the enemy was met in force, wherever they ventured an advance until late in the evening, when Longstreet advanced his line and captured or killed a large number.

This was the last fight of such moment that we had on the north side of the James, though those on the south side, both before and after, were very active. The Battle of Reams' Station,[14] where in late August we inflicted a heavy defeat, was a very severe and important battle, checking for a long time Grant's extension to our right. Mahone, too, made several attacks on their line, twice bringing out more prisoners than he had men, besides inflicting heavy losses on the enemy in killed and wounded.

When the Spring opened, Grant had worn our men to the breaking point. With many times our number he forced us to extend so, that our line was only a thin skirmish line at most points. Still he extended, and sent Sheridan to and beyond our right until finally they broke through and the end came. A. P. Hill, who commanded the Third Corps, was killed far inside our lines by the enemy, who had come in through a gap and were a mile inside our lines in heavy force.[15] The day before Colonel W. J. Pegram [16] fell mortally wounded. He was probably, at the time of his death, the most distinguished artillerist in our army. Pelham had been killed more than a year before, being the only officer in the artillery who stood higher, and he not in the estimation of all.

I have always thought that Pelham is justly entitled to first place. He was the first who ever demonstrated that artillery could and should be fought on the musketry line of battle. After he demonstrated it, Pegram and some others fought their guns just as close and just as hard; but no harder than Pelham, who was, as a fighter, not only the pioneer, and if not the most desperate fighter of artillery, certainly the equal of any.

Pelham was a West Pointer, graduating just as the war broke out in the class with Rosser [17] and Young, [18] major generals on the Southern side, and Custer, [19] on the Northern. He early distinguished himself by fighting close and hard, but he was not a good organizer or disciplinarian, and seldom had his command in good condition. If he had been confined for his supply of horses to those drawn through the quartermasters' department, he would have been scarcely ever able to transport half his guns. But moving constantly with the cavalry and always at the front, his command picked up fresh horses and equipment, which never passed through the hands of the department.

Even with his extra supply, he was often unable to move all his guns when he wanted, but his rule was to go ahead when fighting was to be done and to wait for no stragglers. He went right in with whatever could keep up, and the fighting spirit of his men was such that most of them came up as quickly as they could and joined right in. His officers were all instructed by him, and Breathed, McGregor, Thomson, Chew, and Henry [20] were all noted as fighters. When he fell in a rather small fight on the Rappahannock, Pelham left behind a number of unsurpassed artillerymen, who had been thoroughly trained by him. And his Horse Artillery was noted until the end as dashing and effective fighters.

Pegram, whom some thought Pelham's superior, was utterly different. A student at the University of Virginia when the war started, he had no experience in any branch of the military. Brought up in the city of Richmond, he was apparently as unfitted for army life as one could well be. Awkward in figure, so nearsighted as to be helpless without his glasses, a poor horseman (he could hardly distinguish the horse he rode for years from any other), he was as little intended for a soldier as history tells us Wolfe, the hero of Quebec, was. But he was every whit Wolfe's equal in high character, and in the estimate of many was the best officer of artillery in the Army of Northern Virginia.

I was Pegram's very close friend, and we were thrown much together in the winter of '63–'64, when our camps were close together. We were about the same age, much younger than the other battalion commanders, and the better I knew him the greater my wonder was to see how he could overcome his natural defects. But he did; and altogether because he had a character and will that were grand, a sense of duty, never surpassed, and a determination to do his best, utterly regardless of his own safety or comfort.

Pegram's force of character and iron courage brought him into notice. As a cool, desperate fighter, who regardless of danger or odds, never thought of giving way, he stood as high, possibly higher, as any man in the army. He fell, resisting the charge that broke our lines at the end, and died as grandly as he had lived, without a murmur of regret except that he could do no more. He was one of the most earnest Christians I ever met, and when death came, it had no terror for him.

Chapter 7

The Exhaustion of Retreat

WHEN the Sunday that saw our line so broken we were ordered to draw off from our positions on the north side of the river came, I was at Drewry's Bluff, dining with Major Hampton Gibbes, the commandant there, and his wife. We knew that fighting was going on below Petersburg, but it had been so constant for months that we thought little of it until a courier came, bringing me a dispatch which General Ewell had received from General Lee and had sent to all the officers having commands.[1] It was to the effect that all our troops, where not in line, were to be marched toward Richmond. The quartermasters were to get all wagons ready and, as far as possible, loaded with forage and supplies. The commissaries were to get and to issue rations to all the troops. Those men and guns, which were too near the enemy to be moved without being seen, were as soon as dark came, to be brought out and sent to Richmond.

I at once sent couriers to all my officers in accordance with these orders, and went myself to overlook the movement. When I got to my camp, about nine o'clock that night, I found everything packed. Soon the guns and men, who had moved after dark, got in and received the rations which had been prepared for them, and we started for Richmond about ten o'clock.

I had some time before been fortunate enough to find a bootmaker in Richmond who had gotten some very fine leather through the blockade. He had made me a pair of boots, although refusing to let me have more than one pair, for which I paid him twelve hundred and fifty dollars. They were so new that they were not very comfortable, and I took them off when I reached camp. I then put them with some other valued possessions in an ambulance. I sent it with a battery of Armstrong's guns, which had been assigned me but never put on the permanent line, as they were held too valuable and were only sent out for some special service where their great, accurate range and English ammunition could do work that justified risking them.[2]

The battery's captain was ordered to cross the river at Richmond and wait on the other side, but when he got there he decided to follow his own lead. He went off after some infantry to find a better place and drove straight into the enemy's lines, losing my cherished Armstrong guns and my twelve hundred dollar boots. When I got to Richmond, everything was in the wildest confusion. I met my quartermaster just below the town with a lot of much needed horses; one fine pair he had found in a drygoods store behind the counter. The low characters of the town had broken into everything, gotten a lot of whiskey, and were looting the place, being aided to a considerable extent by the soldiers, who had broken through all discipline. As I rode by the principal jewelry store, I saw an old woman come crawling backward out of a window. One of the mounted men rode up and whacked her with the flat of his sword. She tumbled out with a yell, and her lapful of plunder from the showcases of Mitchell and Tyler, the leading jewelers of Richmond, poured over the sidewalk. At another store, a party was beating in the door, which burst in only to show the owner armed. He fired on his assailants, one of whom fell, but instantly he was himself shot to death.

A crowd of plunderers filled the Government warehouses down at the bridge. There was a large amount of whiskey in one house, just at the bridge, and the plunderers, filled with it, were throwing out everything they could lay their hands on, utterly regardless of the crowd below. Numbers were crushed by the large bags and boxes and barrels, thrown from the third and fourth stories. No one seemed to pay the slightest heed or attention, but would rush in to plunder as soon as anything was thrown out, though it might have crushed to death someone an arm's length away. This went on as long as I was there, which was for hours as I waited to see the men and guns across.

In the intervals caused by the passing of other commands between the different detachments of mine, I rode to the houses to say goodby to many, who had been as kind as if my nearest kin. First among them were the Dudleys, who were as devoted as my own parents and brothers and sisters could ever have been. I owed my life to them and Dr. Gibson. So utterly was everything broken and wrecked, and so hard was the struggle, which was left, to those who survived, that this was as utter a severance and parting from all these as death itself; and many of them I never saw again.

When, after many years, I saw Richmond again, none of either of these families, to whom I owed so much, was there. All were dead except Thomas Dudley, from whom I parted at Appomattox. As a major and assistant to the Commissary General, he spent the night after Appomattox at our last campfire, in which he burned many thousand dollars of Confederate currency, with some of which he had tried to buy provisions on the road and had in some cases succeeded. Each of us took specimens of the different bills as mementos (I have mine still).

He was the last of his father's family, but when I stood

looking at the house, which for four years was a home as open to me as our own, he was a bishop and living in Louisville, Kentucky. Next door was Dr. Gibson's house, where I was almost as much at home, and where Dr. Gibson had had me carried that he might give me all the attention needed, by being with me even while he rested from attending to other sick and wounded, too many for any one man, yet which he did thoroughly and well. He, too, as well as his wife, who helped also those his skill saved, was dead, when I was in Richmond again, and his daughter, whom I remembered as a favorite in wartime society, was in New York, making a brave fight for her orphaned children. I met Bishop Dudley once on a passing train, but that is all I have seen of these dearest friends in the thirty-odd years that have passed since that night.

To return to the night we left the lines before Richmond, when I got home from Major Gibbes' place, I called my servant, Willis, who had been with me for three years. I had hired him, when my groom was taken sick, and some months later he came to me one day and asked me to buy him. He said that he was owned by an estate, the heirs of which were children, that he was hired out all the time, and wanted a settled home. I very willingly bought him, as he was a faithful and efficient fellow, the best groom I ever saw. In time, he did everything for me, and regarded himself as more of a guardian than a servant. When I was wounded in '64, he was in almost as quickly as the litter-bearers, and stayed under fire to attend to me. As soon as he found that I was not killed, he began to abuse me for taking his favorite mare under fire. He never did quite forgive me for allowing—at Cold Harbor—the killing of the horse which he would without hesitation have backed against a Derby winner for all he owned.

I told him that we were evacuating, and I wanted to know if he was going with me or intended to leave me. I told him to think it over and to let me know. After supper, he said that he wanted to stay, as he had been married only a week—about the tenth time since I had owned him—and did not think that he could part with his wife so soon. I told him all right, and gave him a share of the small supply of gold I had. When we got to Richmond, I told him to turn the mare, which he was riding, over to my orderly. He was weeping bitterly and finally said that he could not leave me and the mare, but if I would let him go to see his wife, he would join me in the morning at Manchester, where I had been ordered to camp. But when I got across the river I was ordered on at once and never heard of Willis again.

When I got to Richmond, years later, I could get no trace of him. I was recognized by the headwaiter of one of the hotels—he had been the body-servant of Surgeon-General Moore [3] of the Confederate Army—and asked him to try to trace Willis. When next I saw him he said that he had heard that Willis had tried to follow me, but could not and had been captured by the Yankees. He had been forced into the service of some Union general, and finally went north with a racing stable. I always thought, however, that the headwaiter made it all up in his desire to oblige me. He was very bitter about the taking away of colored servants by Northerners and thought there should be a law to forbid it. "Why, sir," he said, "they are so anxious to do like old-time Southern gentlemen, they take my waiters before they know the difference between a platter and a dish."

On getting into my camp from the front the night after leaving Richmond, I found sitting at my campfire my brother Lewis, the seventh of the family who had enlisted. [4] He had just got in from South Carolina to join the army, with a sore-back horse, which we found could be ridden without touching the sore by using my saddle. It was a very handsome McClellan, which had been taken from Custer on the morning Fitz Lee captured much of his personal property and the correspondence, which was published in the *Richmond Examiner* and has been discussed much since. The saddle was taken by one of Lee's orderlies, and my friend, Major Mason,[5] Lee's adjutant general, got it from him for me.

I had fastened on the saddle my leather bag, which held a number of things I valued, among them over two hundred dollars in gold, which I had gotten by the assistance of Mr. William Cameron [6] of Petersburg, president of a very successful blockade company and a most hospitable entertainer of Confederate officers. One day I was dining with him, when he said that as president of the company he had the right to send out a certain number of bales of cotton for private account, and that he usually transferred the right to friends. He offered General Mahone the privilege of one, one to me, and one each to several others.

In due time each adventurer received between two and three hundred dollars, and my share, almost intact, hung on the saddle which I put on Lewis' horse. As Willis had left me, I detailed a little fellow named Winkler, who had been in one of the companies only a few weeks to ride with Lewis and to act as courier (he is now quite a prominent professional man in New York). After several days of the retreat, I found these boys more worn out than I was, and one night I rode with them several miles ahead until we got to a thicket of scrub pines. Taking them well in, I enjoined them to sleep one at a time, with the other standing guard and each tying his horse to his wrist.

I rode back to the battalion and for the next two hours was skirmishing with Sheridan's cavalry, which gave us no rest, day or night. I had left word for my wagons to halt at a point near where I had left the boys and to cook supper. The last halt I was directed to make was about three-quarters of a mile from where I was to have my supper. I sat at the root of a tree, holding my horse, and went fast asleep, with the skirmishing going on all around me. Finally my orderly, whom I had managed to let have some rest, rescued me and told me that the enemy was right on us, as our skirmishers had fallen back. I got up, and looking over the little creek bottom saw a loose horse. I sent Chadwick, my orderly, to catch it. He did so, and I rode toward where the wagons were to be.

When I got to the thicket, I went in to call Lewis and his companion but found it occupied by sleeping members of a brigade, who resented my efforts to find Lewis and Winkler most vigorously. At last, when about to give up, I stumbled on them. But the horse with the gold was gone, Lewis having failed to tie him as I had told him, and with Winkler having promptly gone to sleep. With a much discouraged appetite I went to supper, and when I had finished I had Chadwick to bring his capture to the light to see if he could be a substitute for Tramp, Lewis' horse. When it came into the light, it turned out to be Tramp, himself, with not a single thing missing. When Chadwick picked him up in the dark, he was within fifty yards of the enemy's skirmish line.

The day after we left Richmond there was a kind of re-arrangement of the army; Longstreet was put in command of the rear and given some informally organized artillery commands, which he ordered me to take charge of. General Alexander was his chief of artillery; but as he had done duty as corps chief for a long time before he was given the rank and title, now he was doing the work of chief for the whole army, again without either the name or place. But he performed as always with all his might and main, and ignored that he was doing work for which he had not the position he should have.[7]

I kept one of the battalions at the rear constantly supplied with men and horses, as the work thinned the others. This constant effort tired me as I would never have imagined one could be tired. I felt sometimes as if I could not sit on my horse another minute. I have heard men say that they could sleep on their horses, but I never could. I would go to sleep for a second only, to start up the next second to save myself, a most agonizing feeling and not restful. At times I would get off my horse, sit down, and be instantly asleep. I would have to be shakened to be awakened, even when firing was going on. From my previous experience I would have said that this was impossible, for there are few things more thoroughly wakening than the firing of even a skirmish line.

Day and night we were attacked by Sheridan's men. Whenever we halted to drive off our assailants, they were quickly and heavily reinforced, so we would have hard fighting, often getting the worst of it, losing men as prisoners besides the killed and wounded. In addition, men began to get hopeless as we left their homes behind and dropped out in great numbers. Those who stayed showed great pluck. For days they were without rest or food, except for the scant supplies that we could get on the road.

The night before we reached Appomattox we were not molested for hours, and believed we had got away from the pursuing army. About sunset General Lee passed me and seemed in good spirits, telling me that we had got rid of them, and that we could rest and cook; also that we could take whatever we could find to eat. We halted and set the men to foraging. They killed hogs and cattle, of which there were quite a number, and prepared for a barbecue. In about an hour after I fell asleep, I was waked and told that orders had come to move on. We could hear the cannon a few miles ahead and soon found that Sheridan, with better information than General Lee, had moved by a shorter road from Farmville and was in line across our route to Appomattox.

We marched until daylight and then began to fight on the hill at Appomattox. Gordon occupied the first line, and Longstreet took a position about a mile from the village in supporting distance. An hour or possibly a little more after daylight, Longstreet told me that Gordon had called for support, especially artillery. He directed me to take three batteries and to go to the front to give such help as I could, and authorized me to call on any infantry to furnish me with support.

I went just beyond Appomattox Court House and opened fire on the enemy. As I moved to position, I called on General Benning,[8] who commanded a brigade of Georgians, Toombs' old brigade of Hood's old division, to support my guns. He took two regiments and went forward, taking a position near that in which I placed the guns.

For some time the firing was light, but soon the enemy's skirmishers came close, accompanied by several new batteries, so that I began to find that we were overmatched. I called on the infantry to keep down the skirmishers, which they did promptly. But when a new battery came in and opened on us, I could not reply, as we already had all we could attend to. I appealed to the Georgians again to help, expecting them to annoy the battery with sharpshooters. Instead, they dashed forward so fast that they captured the battery, giving the company such scant time to get away that it left the guns, horses, and every other piece of equipment in perfect condition. We had only to put drivers on the horses and to get men to man the guns to have the best equipped battery in our army, and to have it firing on its owners of but a few minutes before. It turned out later that it was fresh from Washington and was having its first experience in the field. Its captain told me, in tears, when he got it back, stripped of its fine horses and equipment, that it was the crack battery of the army.

About this time a staff officer rode up and gave me an order from General Gordon to cease firing. As I declined to recognize an order from anyone but Longstreet or someone superior to him, the officer rode away to report. In a few minutes Gordon, himself, rode up. With him was Colonel Venable of General Lee's staff, who told me that General Lee had ridden to meet General Grant and the fight was over.

On hearing this, I drew my guns out and rode back to

Longstreet, who confirmed it. He told me to remain, as he might have some orders for me, but I told him that I would make my way to Johnston's army. He said to me: "General Lee has agreed to demand terms that I do not believe Grant will give, and I will take nothing else. I know my corps will follow me, and I know we can get through, though we may have a hard time. You," he said, "have the best equipped body of artillery left. How will you feel if it, with the rest of the corps, fights its way through, and you are away from it?"

Of course, after this, I could only tell those, with whom I promised to go that I would not. Most of them decided to stay, only a few of them leaving with General M. W. Gary.[9] They got through without any interference from the enemy, but Grant agreed to General Lee's demands, so neither party's move made the slightest difference.[10]

A staff officer dashed up about this time and gave General Longstreet a message. He at once called to me and, walking aside, told me that I must catch General Lee, if possible, before he got to Grant. I should say to him that Fitz Lee reported he had broken the enemy's line and we could get through readily. He urged me to ride rapidly without sparing my horse. I started at once on a very fast, thoroughbred mare, whose speed was the reason of my selection. I went at full speed for over two miles, going by General Lee suddenly at a sharp turn in the road and into a group of the enemy just beyond him. He had found that Grant was in front with Sheridan, and was only communicating with him through those he met, of whom General Humphreys [11] was, I believe, the ranking officer.

I stopped as quickly as I could and turning back jumped off my horse close to General Lee. As I touched the ground he caught hold of me and taking me off to one side and showing great excitement asked: "What is the matter? What is the matter?"—repeating it two or three times. As soon as I could speak I replied, "General Longstreet says——," and I gave him the message.

He was still greatly disturbed and asked, "Wouldn't he go?" Then, catching himself, he said, "I am afraid Fitz is deceiving himself," and asked me if I had been beyond Appomattox. On my telling him yes, he said, "Could you tell if you were fighting infantry?" I told him there was certainly some infantry, as we had captured some and a battery which belonged to the Fifth Corps. "Yes, yes," he said, "Fitz has fooled himself." Then stepping up to my mare, he said: "Oh, colonel, I am afraid you have ruined your beautiful mare. It is a pity." He patted her and suggested that I should loosen her girths. He then turned to Colonel Marshall [12] of his staff and said that he wanted to get a message to Longstreet as soon as possible. Marshall answered that his horse was lame and John—General Lee's personal courier—reported his horse in the same condition. I suggested that I carry the reply. General Lee said: "I will have to accept your offer, but don't ride hard. There is nothing to it." Telling me to tell Longstreet to use his own judgment, he again enjoined me not to ride too hard, and I left him. I had only gone a short distance when I met Colonel Fairfax of Longstreet's staff. He had been sent to tell General Lee that the report was all wrong; that Fitz Lee had only gone through an advance line of cavalry. [13]

When I got back Longstreet was standing just where I had left him. I gave him General Lee's message to act on his own judgment in any emergency. Just then a Union officer came dashing up with Major Gibbes. He was a most striking picture: a rather young man, dressed in a blue sack with the largest shoulder-straps of a major general I ever saw; with long, red hair hanging in oily curls down near to his shoulders, a gorgeous red scarf in which there was a gold pin, nearly two inches in length and breadth, with big letters, "George A. Custer, Major General."

As Custer swaggered up to Longstreet, he called out so

loud that all around must hear, "I have come to demand your instant surrender. We are in a position to crush you and unless you surrender at once we will destroy you."

Longstreet said: "By what authority do you come into our lines? General Lee is in communication with General Grant. We certainly will not recognize any subordinate."

Custer immediately swaggered out, "Oh, Sheridan and I are independent of Grant and we will destroy you if you don't surrender at once."

Longstreet answered: "I suppose you know no better and have violated the decencies of military procedure because you know no better. But your ignorance will not save you if you do so again. Now go, and act as you and Sheridan choose; and I will teach you a lesson you won't forget." Then raising his voice and shaking his finger, he repeated, "Now, go."

If I ever saw a man with his tail between his legs, it was Custer. He asked for a safeguard back to his own lines, and someone pointed to Colonel Osmun Latrobe, Longstreet's adjutant general. Custer came up to him and asked him for a guard. It appeared that when he came into our lines with a handkerchief in his hand, some of our men pulled him off his horse and handled him rather roughly, though they did not injure him. He saw Major Gibbes, with whom he had been at West Point, and made a most clamorous appeal for protection. It was in that way that Gibbes had happened to bring him to Longstreet.[14]

Custer was mounted on a very inferior horse and when Latrobe gave him a guard, he saw some very handsome horses standing there. At once recovering his self-possession, he expressed a desire for one that happened to be mine. I told him it was not for sale or plunder, and asked him to tell us if Colonel Frank Huger was living, as I noticed that he was wearing Colonel Huger's spurs. They were a very handsome pair of gold-mounted, Mexican spurs, which Santa Anna had worn during the Mexican War and which were given to General Huger, Colonel Frank's father, who was chief of ordinance on Scott's staff. Custer flushed, and said that he had only taken them to care for them for Huger, who had been his friend at West Point. Years after, Colonel Huger told me that he had never been able to get them from Custer who insisted on continuing to take care of them until his death.

Chapter 8

Surrender

To meet Grant, General Lee wore a full new uniform with a very handsome sword, which he had not worn on duty, and was accompanied by only a single staff officer and an orderly. He was gone for perhaps an hour when he rode back and had some talk with Longstreet and some of his staff. Riding past where I happened to be, he stopped and looking me over said, "Have you a decent uniform?" (The one I had on, I had put on in Richmond the week before, and it had been in every kind of mud and rain.) As my wagons had not been captured, I could answer that I had. "Then put it on, sir, and report at my headquarters." [1]

When I did report he told me that I was to take command of the artillery, and should go with Longstreet to arrange for the surrender.[2] I got the artillery together and parked it, and at once the men who had damaged horses and saw better ones came asking to be allowed to trade them. With General Longstreet's approval, I let them take any horses they wanted, putting theirs in place. The first choice was those of our fancy battery from Washington, and in a very short time all the horses, saddles, blankets, valises, and other equipment were replaced by those which had seen much service. Before the trading was finished, however, General Lee rode by, and calling out to me enjoined me to keep everything intact. I told him what had been done, but assured him that nothing more should be disturbed. "Well," he said, "it would have been better if it had not been done, but I am glad, as it has been, that our poor fellows have some benefit."

I went with Longstreet and the rest of the commission to the McLean [3] house, where we met Grant and a number of other officers. Grant greeted Longstreet very cordially—they were at West Point together—and after Longstreet had introduced all of us, Grant turned to General Gibbon, saying to Longstreet, "I will turn you over to General Gibbon and these other gentlemen." I forget most of them, but Griffin,[4] who commanded the Fifth Corps, and Bartlett,[5] a division commander under Griffin, were two of them. Bartlett was the one to whom I turned over the artillery.

Grant and Longstreet talked for some minutes, apparently recalling old times. Then Grant said, "Gentlemen, I have to go to Washington." He told us good day and walked out. Then Longstreet told me to ride back to our army and ask General Lee something, on which Longstreet wanted some information. I went out to my horse, the one I bought in Richmond when I was wounded and lost my arm. When I got there Grant was standing, admiring him. He turned to me and said: "I am admiring your horse. He is very beautiful." After asking a question or two, he said: "I would like very much to have him. Will you sell him?"

When I answered that I would not, he said goodby and turned to mount his horse. Seeing that I had also mounted he said: "Ride with me; I would like to see your horse move." We rode some two hundred yards together to where our roads separated. As we parted, he said again: "Will nothing change your mind about that horse? He is the handsomest I ever saw, and I would greatly like to have him." But I again told him "no," and we parted. I never saw him again, though I was frequently near where he was.

He went over to New York to Farragut's funeral, when he was President, and my father-in-law, General Hampton, then a United States Senator, went as a member of the Senate committee in the same car. They talked of horses and Grant said, "The finest horse I ever saw was ridden by a very young Confederate officer...," he thought a colonel of artillery with one arm, but the horse he described accurately. General Hampton told him I had owned the horse, which was buried on my plantation in the South.

I heard of the horse first from President Davis, when he visited me while I was recovering. Before I ever rode him, General Lee rode him in the Sharpsburg campaign, as his horse was lame, and never forgot him, inquiring about him while on his last visit south. Grant saw and admired him at Appomattox, and fifteen years after remembered and asked after him.

For two days I was kept constantly busy with Bartlett, making out lists and turning over guns and supplies, getting receipts and signing papers for our soldiers. Each of the commission was furnished with blanks to fill in for the troops he represented. I signed a good many hundred and came across a lot of the blanks a short time ago.

Bartlett and I got to be very friendly, and he was very kind in trying to do anything he could for me. He bought another beautiful horse I had, the one I rode to catch General Lee. I had no servant, and as I could not well take more than one horse with me, I parted with a common one and to my great regret with this mare. As Bartlett had been so courteous, when I left I sent him a set of English horse clothing and a bridle. He was delighted with them and wrote me from New York to thank me and to tell me of the mare, and to renew his offers of service. I never saw him again and heard only last winter that he had died a couple of years ago.

The Union troops were very friendly, in fact almost oppressively so, turning out the guard constantly as I would ride by, cheering, and talking to my couriers as though they were the best of friends. I never saw them together for five minutes that the Union soldiers failed to say, "Never mind, boys, we will all get together, and go down with Uncle Bob to lead us and drive the French out of Mexico." One thing greatly struck me: while I heard this dozens of times from Union soldiers, I never heard them fail to add that General Lee was to command. No suggestion was ever made that Grant or any other of their generals should command. It was always General Lee, or as they, with a familiarity greater than most of his men ever showed, called him, Uncle Bob. Once my personal orderly, a fellow of no humor but great pluck, took one of them severely to task for it, and threatened to black his eye if he did it again. For, he stated, "No Yankee has any call to claim him. He is ours."

After I had finished my work with Bartlett I prepared to start home with several friends and my brothers. Lewis had got through the retreat safely, a pretty severe baptism into the service. When all was ready, I rode over to see Colonel Venable and Colonel Taylor [6] of General Lee's staff, to both of whom I was very greatly attached. General Lee's tent was close to theirs, but I did not intend to disturb him, and after telling the others goodby was mounting my horse when I heard my name called and saw General Lee standing in the opening of his tent.

I immediately went to him. He took me in, asked me to sit down, and at once said, "I expect you think I have been very unjust to you." I suppose he referred to his having denied me the promotion to which I was recommended in Johnston's army. I did think so, but mumbled some disclaimer. He went on, "Perhaps I have been, but you have a long life to live and plenty of time to get what you want; and if you ever command an army you will find that try as you may, you can't always do justice." He then asked me what I expected to do, and I told him that I already had offers to go to Brazil, which was then at war with the Argentine Republic. He said, "I will ask you to let me write you a letter which you may find useful." Some time after I received a letter from him, more flattering than I could have expected from anyone. Unfortunately I lost it in a fire with several others which I especially valued. But it gratified me greatly as up to that time he never had said a word that could have been construed as praise or approbation.

I never saw him again, but as I grow older and compare him with other men, he always grows larger and grander. And when I read of the great men of history, I constantly, involuntarily, measure them with him and they shrink in the comparison. There have been generals with more genius, leaders in politics who led their people more; but no man has ever lived who combined greater ability as a soldier, more statesmanlike views, where he had to exercise them, and a grander personality, with the very highest virtue and unselfish devotion to a high sense of duty.

This finishes what I remember. I have written hurriedly and without order. But I have tried to give part of what I saw and lived through, fully recognizing that I have omitted many things which in justice to others should be recorded. I can only give the side of the shield I saw, and that most imperfectly, for after thirty-eight years and writing solely from memory, the most I can hope to have done is not to misstate anything which I include. This I am very sure I have not done. I have stated no fact that I do not know to be true and no opinions that I do not fully believe in; although as to those I may be wrong. I may have done injustice to some by not telling things to their credit. I have not done so intentionally and hope that I have not done so at all. I may some day revise this, but I will probably leave it to my family as it is, to dispose of as they think best.

Appendix

The Haskells

WHEN Fort Sumter became the target for Southern guns, April 12, 1861, six of the eight sons of Charles Thomson and Sophia Lovell (Cheves) Haskell were over eighteen years of age. The four oldest—Langdon, Charles, William, and Alexander—on the secession of their native state, South Carolina, immediately volunteered for service. A fifth, John, quickly made his way to Charleston when he heard of the mounting tension at Sumter and joined the ranks. Before the war was over, two younger boys, Joseph and Lewis, took their places with the troops, leaving only Paul, sixteen at the end of the war, at home with their father, mother, and sisters.

The Haskells had long been Carolinians, and held no reservations about secession. Their ancestral roots were in the low country, on the banks of the Santee River in Amelia Township, St. Mathew's Parish. There the first of their progenitors, the French refugee family of Courtonne, arrived in 1735. Irish, Scotch-Irish, and Scottish blood was added with the coming of the Thomsons of Pennsylvania, Haskells of Massachusetts, and Alexander Cheves of Aberdeenshire, Scotland. Traditions of high deeds in the American Revolution were prevalent in the family folklore to balance the Tory activities of Cheves, but it was the unusual son of the Scottish

Tory who lifted the family out of its previous, purely local prominence.

Langdon Cheves was born in the Bulltown Fort of the Ninety-Six District—it later became the Abbeville District—in the year the nation asserted its independence. Tragic events stalked the family. The Indians killed and scalped the boy's aunt as she tried to reach the farmhouse for necessities for the mother—her sister—and the baby, Langdon. Three years later, Langdon's mother died, and his father, who was an Indian trader, found his life made difficult by his neighbors because of his loyalty to the Crown. In 1782, when the British finally evacuated Charleston, the elder Cheves left his son with relatives on the raw frontier and returned to his native Scotland.

Langdon went to school for a time dressed in "breeches of one leg" (a homespun linen smock) and armed with a stick to beat off snakes. But when he was about nine his father returned to America and soon took him to live in Charleston. With typical frontier spirit Langdon at an early age sought independence. By hard work and study he gained a place for himself in law, politics, and finance. He served in Congress for a short time, and achieved election as Speaker of the House of Representatives. In 1819 he received appointment as Director of the United States Bank and served as its president for three years. He later became Commissioner of Claims under the Treaty of Ghent, but his desire was for the life of a planter, to which he gave his remaining years.

Langdon Cheves had fourteen children, the third of them Sophia Lovell. On December 1, 1830, she married Charles Haskell, and moved to a plantation near Fort Motte, which was close to her father's home. Here, surrounded by a circle of friends and relatives, they lived for several years and here was born their first child, a boy, who was named for his maternal grandfather. At the urging of Langdon Cheves, however, the young couple moved in 1832 to the Abbeville District and the more pleasing climate of the Piedmont hills.

The Haskells bought several places near Davis's Bridge from

people who wished to follow the fortunes of cotton to the distant new lands in Alabama and Mississippi. For the next thirteen years they lived at "The Home Place." When the family outgrew the first house, they built a new one but kept the original name. Oak, pine, and walnut were cut for timbers and brick burned on the plantation for the rambling structure of eight large rooms, two attics, an inviting pantry, and big storeroom. In the yard, about 150 feet away, an outbuilding of two rooms served as a kitchen and tutor's lodging.

Charles Haskell was a cultured, wealthy man who found a full and busy life in running his plantation. In early winter, wagons carried cotton, whiskey and other products some 65 miles to the railroad at Hamburg. There, in turn, the family secured the varied supplies needed, including imports from Europe, for the coming year.

Sophia Haskell, like all plantation wives, had the responsibility for the ill, from the children of the slaves to her own family. A person of high character—kind, tolerant, and generous—she needed all her calm courage to cope with the problems of a growing family. First after Langdon was Mary Elizabeth. Then came Charles Thomson, followed by Charlotte Thomson, who died in infancy, and William Thomson, born in 1837. The sixth child, Alexander Cheves, arrived in 1839, followed by John Cheves in 1841, Joseph Cheves in 1843, and Sophia Louise, whose birthday was Christmas 1845. After the new house was built Lewis Wardlaw, the tenth child, was born in 1847, with Paul Thomson following in 1849 and Hayne Cheves, who died within a few weeks, in 1851.

There was elasticity, typical of the time, about the rambling house. Relatives and friends were welcome in unlimited numbers for visits of varying lengths. In addition to the large family, Robert Hayne Cheves,* youngest of Mrs. Haskell's brothers, lived with

* Robert Cheeves was born in 1829 at "Abbeville," the name given to the Cheves' home in Pennsylvania. He went to South Carolina College and contracted measles, which led to tuberculosis. He died

them for several years. And the children's tutor, who came in 1841, became almost a member of the family. In that year, when the oldest of the children was twelve, some of them found a wayfarer, gaunt and tired, on a nearby road. They led the stranger, who was barefoot and wore a coonskin cap, to the house for food. The impression which he made on the family was such that he stayed on for the next ten years as friend and teacher.

Alban Hart was the newcomer's name. He was the son of an English clergyman and had been a member of the faculty at Chapel Hill, North Carolina. A periodic mental illness explained his wanderings but never detracted from the devotion the Haskells gave him.

He conducted classes in one room of the log building which also held the kitchen. A rough, slanted board desk and a long bench were the schoolroom's chief furnishings. Ink balls which fell from the numerous oaks furnished ink, while geese from the plantation's flocks, amid much furor, gave up feathers for the quills. From his homemade chair and table, Professor Hart, aided or annoyed by Nimrod, his cat, and a little black hen which insisted on laying her eggs in the room, drilled his pupils.

About 1851, when John Cheves was ten, Hart revealed to the family that he was a Jesuit priest, and that his assignment called for him to report to an institution in Alabama. The youngsters literally ran wild after his departure until their parents could secure a new tutor. The Reverend Mr. Green, rector of the Episcopal church at Abbeville, took over the task for a time. Of Irish birth and ordained in the Church of England, he was a "sweet companion for the boys, very little of a preacher but sweet in his life, passionately fond of cigars, rabbit hunting, pleasant company, and two glasses of hot Scotch or Irish on grand occasions." He shortly found the blandishments of a wealthy Philadelphian too tempting to resist and left, to be succeeded by a

---

at nineteen in Florence, Italy, where he had gone in search of health. Langdon Haskell, who was his boyhood companion, was in Italy with him when he died.

"crazy German," who stayed only six months. Without the services of a master, study again became nonexistent. This time, the Haskells solved the problem by sending the boys away to school.

About the first of July each year the Haskells migrated to "The Cabins," which, though only a few miles from the plantation, was higher and free from the malaria which sometimes infested the lower areas. There they shared a tract of some 2,000 acres with friends—the Parkers, Thomases, Palmers, and Calhouns. Other families bought into the group as original members moved away. None of the property was cleared, except for an area around each dwelling, and no attempt to plow or plant it was made, as it was believed that to turn the soil would bring malaria. Slaves swept clean the yards, which made wonderful places in which to play shinny, marbles, and other games.

Everyone in the Haskell household looked forward to the day of the trek to the summer retreat. The servants packed a sufficient supply of staples, such as sugar and coffee, to provide for the whole period. The loaded wagons, piled high with furniture of every sort—beds, piano, chairs, china, glasses, and silver—were pulled by four- or six-horse teams. After the wagon train and the two accompanying milk cows departed, the family, with huge picnic baskets, took places in carriages or on horses and made the journey in comfort.

Three or four happy, carefree months followed. The family kept in weekly touch with "The Home Place," whence came meat, vegetables, butter, meal, and hominy to replenish the larder. The children spent most of the time roaming through the blackjack thickets or among the great oaks and chestnuts. They gathered chinquapins and muscadines, but riding horseback, which all did with ease after early training, was their favorite sport.

Langdon, the eldest, was naturally the first to enter college. In 1847, at the age of sixteen, he enrolled in South Carolina College at Columbia. The sensitive and rather nervous youth was the smallest in stature of the brothers, something which possibly contributed to his romantic temperament. Though sometimes given to gloom and despair he was usually bright and socially charming. Because of his dark complexion and black hair, he was given the nickname "The Indian." When he graduated, he was still much too young to enter a profession, so he spent the next two years leisurely reading law. After his admission to the bar he practiced in Abbeville for a time but in 1856 moved to Charleston, where the attractive life in a cosmopolitan society appealed to him. After a trip abroad he married Ella Wardlaw, whose family were close friends of the Haskells, and moved with her to Arkansas.

The second son bore the name of his father, Charles Thomson Haskell. He was large in size, generous and impulsive. When it was time for him to start college, the country was still in the grip of the martial spirit the Mexican War had created. Influenced by this feeling, Charles chose a military school, the Citadel, and after graduation became a construction engineer for the North Eastern Railroad, then being built between Charleston and Florence, South Carolina. In 1860 he was engaged in engineering work in Mississippi.

William Thomson, the third son, was away at school in Charleston by the time he was fourteen. Willy, the pet name the family gave him, was difficult and unruly, but after his recovery from a serious attack of pneumonia in Charleston he became a changed personality. "All the force of his nature went to overcome evil, and to the end he was the most perfect character I have ever known," wrote his brother Alexander of him. He entered the University of Virginia in 1856, and though not a brilliant student, he overcame his scholastic difficulties, was chosen editor of the college magazine and gained recognition as a skilled orator. After graduation William, like Langdon, studied law and was about to enter this profession when war came.

In the spring of 1854 tragedy struck the family when Mary, one of its most cherished members, died. After her death Alexander, known in his youth as Ecky and Cotton Head but later as Aleck, was sent away to school before he was fifteen. He was a nervous, timid lad, who stuttered badly but had a vivid, tenacious memory and a great zest for life. While at school in Charleston he prepared for his examinations at South Carolina College with such intensity that he qualified for admission in 1856. But he had taxed his health by his long hours of study and caught malaria, which kept him long in ill health. His illness almost prevented his joining an extended camping and fishing trip into the Blue Ridge Mountains with three of his brothers and a friend. But he did go, and the sun and healthy outdoor life completed his cure. This type of rugged experience hardened the boys and enabled them to endure the hardships of future military life.

At the time Aleck was a junior his brother John also entered South Carolina College. When John was three years old, he had been desperately ill with whooping cough which, according to the family tradition, stunted his growth. By the same account it was garlic alone, administered as a medicine, which saved his life. When John entered college he and Aleck became, and remained, roommates until Aleck's graduation.

After commencement, which came as the college term ended for the Christmas vacation, Aleck and John went to Abbeville where they met William, who had graduated at Charlottesville the summer before. Seasonal activities proceeded as usual, but constantly in the background was the furor which accompanied the secession of the state. When the three boys announced their intention to volunteer for service with the company of infantry Captain Perrin was raising, their father firmly pointed out to John that he should return to his studies at the start of the new college term. Only Aleck and William reported as recruits for Company D, First South Carolina Volunteers.

As the Confederacy was then not in existence, these were troops of the independent government of South Carolina. Colonel Maxcy Gregg, a prominent lawyer of Columbia, who had long been an ardent secessionist and was a member of the South Carolina Convention, was the regiment's commanding officer. Although in 1846 he had received a commission as major in a regiment of volunteers for the Mexican War, he had seen no active service, but he still had more experience in the command of troops than the majority of his fellows. He proved an able military commander, and as a cultured man, deeply interested in astronomy, botany, and ornithology, and a student of the Greek drama and philosophy, he had great influence on young Aleck Haskell in the years of the war.

The two Haskell brothers on January 8, 1861, arrived in Charleston just two weeks before the United States garrison had moved from Fort Moultrie to Fort Sumter. This concentration caused the South Carolina leaders to sweep all caution aside. The next day enthusiastic Carolinians raised the flag of the Palmetto State over Moultrie and other works the Union forces had abandoned. Quickly they turned to strengthening and fitting these positions for the use of the state's troops. They pushed their preparations with vigor, and on January 9 they felt confident enough to fire on the flag of the United States, which flew above the *Star of the West,* an unarmed merchant ship sent to deliver men, arms and supplies to the Fort Sumter garrison.

It was in the midst of this excitement that the Haskells reported for duty with Captain Perrin's company of Gregg's Regiment. The roster of the hastily organized unit read like a social register of the state. It included 27 physicians, 30 lawyers, and the most prominent among the young planters and businessmen, and was an outfit of which its members were intensely proud. Dressed in red shirts, black pants, and minutemen's caps, they joined the work gangs as soon as they arrived. Shovels, wheelbarrows, and surcingles proved to be the amateur soldiers' first tools of war, and were a bit embarrassing when it was necessary to salute a superior officer, while the necessity to ignore onetime social rank in an observance of soldierly duty also created occasional difficulty.

But in the enthusiasm of the moment everyone rejoiced in performing any task, however exhausting or menial. While he labored to raise the embankments of Fort Moultrie, Aleck again met the Virginian Edmond Ruffin, whom he had first seen the preceding year at a student rally for secession. The old warrior stopped him as he pushed a wheelbarrow and embraced him.

Then nothing would do but that Aleck must allow the aging gentleman to grasp the handles of the wheelbarrow and the two pushed the load up the wooden ramp to the spot where they dumped the earth.

In mid-February Aleck Haskell was elevated to a staff position as military secretary to Colonel Gregg. Although not a commissioned officer he had the uniform and sword of the rank and enjoyed the privilege of living at the colonel's quarters.

Early in March the growing tenseness of the situation at Charleston received recognition by the Confederacy when the newly formed government ordered General Pierre G. T. Beauregard to that area to assume command of all troops—regulars, militia, and volunteers—on duty there. In the growing force which the dapper Louisianian found, there were two more members of the Haskell family: Langdon, who had come on from his Arkansas plantation to take service as a volunteer aide with Colonel Gregg, and Charles, whose training at the Citadel and experience as an engineer won him rank as a lieutenant and an assignment as a staff officer with Colonel R. H. Anderson, who was in command on Sullivan's Island. John, too, joined the forces in Charleston harbor before the first guns of war were fired.

With Sumter past, the five brothers began to separate under the necessities of their military duties. Charles, Langdon, and John remained in their posts at Charleston. William and Alexander moved to Virginia with a regiment of infantry under Colonel Gregg, but they missed the action at First Manassas. Shortly, John and Langdon also received orders to move to Virginia. Only Charles was left at Charleston, although for a time those who were with Gregg—William, Alexander, and Langdon—returned to South Carolina for a reorganization and to seek recruits.

Gregg's Brigade remained on the South Carolina coast until spring 1862, when orders came for it to proceed to Virginia. Now all hoped that their previous bad luck in not getting into any important action would change. But the brigade was not involved in the engagement known both as Seven Pines and Fair Oaks.

However, John, who still suffered from illness, performed some courier service, and Joseph, who was just past his nineteenth birthday and had recently joined the army, won the commendation of his brother. "Joe is a very gallant looking soldier," Aleck said in a letter home, "and must have behaved well. He was at General Johnston's side when the General fell, and will probably be out of employment for some time in consequence of the General's illness." Within a short time, though, Joseph was at work as adjutant of E. P. Alexander's battalion of artillery.

Aleck was ill when the series of engagements known as the Seven Days took place, and John received his severest wound of the war in the second of them. Although Gregg's Brigade was engaged in heavy fighting, both Langdon and William came through unscathed, and Langdon won the praise of the divisional commander, A. P. Hill, for "conspicuous gallantry." In the army reorganization which followed the Seven Days, Gregg's Brigade, as a unit of Hill's Light Division, became part of the command of Jackson. Langdon, who acted as Gregg's A. A. G., in place of Aleck, still ailing, and William with the infantry—"Jackson's foot cavalry"—soon discovered what campaigning with Stonewall was like. In quick succession there were the action at Cedar Mountain, a raid on the enemy's rear, and the brilliant tactical success of Second Manassas. At Second Manassas, it was William who won praise from his superiors for his leadership at a crucial moment in the battle.

In the following September all the Haskells then in Virginia except John, who was still convalescing from the loss of his arm, took part in the invasion of Maryland. Aleck later recalled having seen the elderly Barbara Frietchie, proudly waving her little Union flag as the Confederates made their way through Frederick. It was Gregg's Brigade, with Aleck Haskell in direct charge, which received the surrender of the Federals at Harper's Ferry. Then they hurried on to arrive at Sharpsburg in time to engage in the last of the fighting there.

The Southerners recrossed the Potomac the next day, and as both armies were in urgent need of rest and reorganization, campaigning ceased. In the interlude Aleck gave some of his views on soldiering to those at home. "The range of vision is singularly contracted and circumscribed in the army," he said in one of his letters. "We see but little and foresee nothing. We pitch into fights, and those that come out go quietly on in the hard work of marches, or the routine of camp, and really enjoy the army life with all its painful accessories."

All the Haskells with the Army of Northern Virginia were at Fredericksburg, although John, with a specially constructed empty sleeve for his jacket, performed little service. Gregg's Brigade was under heavy fire, but William and Langdon escaped injury. Aleck was not so lucky, although he did not leave the field until forced to by loss of blood and exhaustion. This time it was Joseph who won commendation. "My especial thanks are . . . due to Confederate States Cadet Joseph C. Haskell," E. P. Alexander said in the report he made after Fredericksburg, "who volunteered me his services and rendered me indispensable assistance in the supervision of so extensive a command. I beg to recommend him to the War Department for promotion."

Aleck returned home to recuperate from his wound, and while in South Carolina took advantage of this opportunity to return to the scenes of his earliest military experience in Charleston harbor. There he visited his brother Charles, who was on duty at one of the forts, and his uncle Langdon Cheves, who as an engineer was busy with the construction of Fort Wagner. About mid-February Aleck was again sufficiently well to rejoin his unit in camp on the Rappahannock River. At Camp Gregg, the name the brigade gave it in memory of their leader, killed at Fredericksburg, Aleck faced squarely in a letter to his mother the probability that death would strike one or more of the brothers in the great struggle which was steadily increasing in intensity. But in other letters he dwelt on the lighter side as when he wrote: "Soldiers in winter quarters are very much like bears in the like situation;

perfect quiet and tranquil repose broken only by the stated periods when the paws must be sucked."

But it was not all monotony: Langdon and William were still in the brigade, and other relatives and friends were nearby with whom they could have an occasional chat or a less frequent cup of coffee, with sugar, if they were lucky. The winter was followed by a cold, wet spring. Then as April turned to May the armies prepared for another season of campaigning. In the first major action, that of Chancellorsville, Aleck received a wound in his left ankle. "When hit, my feet went up in the air, it seemed higher than my head," he said, when describing the incident. The painful injury completely disabled him for a time, but it brought one welcome moment. As he left the field he encountered William, with whom he talked for a few minutes. As at Second Manassas, William won commendation at Chancellorsville from his brigade and regimental commanders for his "efficient" direction of a line of skirmishers and "his accustomed coolness and daring."

In the movement of the Army of Northern Virginia into Pennsylvania in June 1863, four of the Haskells marched with their units. Aleck had not recovered from his wound, so he remained behind. Langdon and Joseph were in their usual staff positions with McGowan, who had succeeded Gregg, and Alexander. John had just joined Longstreet's corps as an artilleryman, and William had a new assignment, command of a group of carefully selected marksmen to act as sharpshooters and skirmishers. But when the battle-weary Confederates made their way back to Virginia, William remained behind. As he led his men forward in the action of the second day at Gettysburg, he received wounds from which he died on the field.

Captain William Haskell had served through all campaigns after First Manassas and according to reports had never been absent from his unit except for a single month in the winter of 1863 when, under orders, he went to South Carolina to round up absentees from the brigade. Major Joseph A. Englehard, A. A. G. of Pender's Division, voiced the opinion of all Willy's comrades in his report of the battle. "This brave and worthy young officer," he stated, "fell while boldly walking along the front line of his command, encouraging his men and selecting favorable positions for them to defend. He was educated and accomplished, possessing in a high degree every virtuous quality of the true gentleman and Christian. He was an officer of most excellent judgment, and a soldier of the coolest and most chivalrous daring."

The entire brigade felt a serious loss in the death of Captain Haskell. In camp he had the reputation of being a thorough yet discriminating disciplinarian, and in action all singled him out for his high spirit and complete self-possession. Late in July Aleck wrote home: "Of Willy I hear daily praise and affectionate comment, as though he was still among us. I have never seen such a case. The Brigade mourn his loss more than that of any man who has ever fallen in it, more even it seems than that of General Gregg. This for one so humble in rank has rarely been seen. His own Battalion of Sharpshooters almost worship his memory and will never forget him on the field of battle. By our lamented General of Division, the noble Pender who fell in the same battle, Willy was placed amongst his very first officers, and as a man he held a special place in [Pender's] regard. From all sides, Generals and others of the Division have taken occasion to speak to me in terms of the highest admiration of his excellence as an officer and his noble character as a man. All that a soldier could win in a glorious death has been heaped upon him."

Among the family Willy held the most adored place, but as Aleck pointed out to his mother and father, all the brothers had become more attached to each other by their experiences in the war. "Since we have been away from home," Aleck said in a touching letter, "and so often meeting death together and only one another to lean upon, the bonds of love between us brothers have become so close, knit with feelings so tender that now, when broken from my nearest and most intimate, my heart is sadly torn."

Three of the sorrowing brothers were together on July 18, when Aleck wrote home that Langdon and John had come to see him, "both poor fellows much grieved." By that time additional sad tidings had come from South Carolina, where in a Federal attack on Morris Island both their brother Charles and their uncle Langdon Cheves had been killed. Nor was there the alleviation of active service, for after the return of Lee's army from Pennsylvania there was little fighting, and the Confederate lines on the Rapidan reflected the depression of defeat and the barren monotony of inactivity.

Early in September the high command decided to send the infantry of Longstreet's corps with some of its artillery to reinforce Bragg's army in the neighborhood of Chattanooga. Although John Haskell prepared to go, orders held him in Virginia, but brother Joe did make the journey with E. P. Alexander's staff. He was the only Haskell to participate in the war in the western theater, and from the mountaintop of Lookout in Tennessee he observed the beauty of the country, which even human conflict could not obscure, and reflected on the way the massive totality of the mountain scaled down the size and portent of even the forces of the enemy, as they gathered in the valley for their final great effort to relieve their comrades, penned in Chattanooga after the battle of Chickamauga.

Summer 1863 turned to fall and then came a dreary Virginia winter with snow and cold an additional hardship for the men, whose rations were short and other supplies virtually nonexistent. Aleck again suffered a recurrence of his old malaria and in a letter home expressed a hope for some cure to drive away the "ghost of the Rappahannock ague which wracked my bones a few nights ago." He received some compensation from the nearness of John, whose camp was but a short distance away. "Having nothing on my table," he told his mother and father, "(or rather on the table that I have not got) that I could prevail upon myself to swallow, I went over to test John's housekeeping and found such a breakfast as I believe restored me more than quinine."

John was not the only one to offer relief for Aleck's indisposition and boredom, as General Lee also invited him for a meal. In describing his visit with the army commander, Aleck said to his family in Abbeville: "I dined with General Lee this evening and he wished for some red pepper. Send me a box for him, and let it be strong. The General looks well in health, and seems to be in his usual serene good spirits. He becomes a little sarcastic and savage upon men sometimes, but he never quarrels with fate."

With Langdon Aleck attended church "and had the happiness of kneeling, at least two of us together, at the Communion Table." Such interludes served to take Aleck's mind from his growing desire to get away from staff work into active service. A welcome leave of absence at Christmas enabled him to spend the season in Abbeville, and it was not until early February that he returned to his duties. He found a subdued but obvious enthusiasm in camp as the campaigning season again approached, and for him before too long there was good news. On April 28 he heard that he had been commissioned a lieutenant colonel. The commission and his orders to join the 7th Regiment South Carolina Cavalry reached him May 2.

Before Aleck Haskell had settled into his new position, the Federals began the fateful campaign of 1864. But three of the Haskells were in the opening phases of the fighting in the Wilderness. Langdon with McGowan's brigade was in the thick of the action. It began on the morning of May 4, when directions came to prepare cooked rations, but marching orders arrived before the men could complete their task. They threw the half-cooked dough or raw meal into their knapsacks and moved to meet the advancing enemy as the latter became entangled in the scrub and forest of the Wilderness. In the early afternoon scouts ran upon what they thought to be enemy cavalry, but when Langdon and some other officers rode to intercept them, the Federals, who later proved to have been a few misdirected couriers, turned and fled. The episode delighted the men in the ranks, who pushed on into the heavy undergrowth with cheers for the somewhat embarrassed heroes.

Within a day Longstreet's Corps strengthened the Confederates, and with it came two other Haskells, John with his battalion and Joseph with E. P. Alexander's staff. While the three—Langdon, John and Joseph—attended to their tasks in the heavy fighting from May 4 to the middle of the month, Aleck with his regiment had been with Beauregard, who faced the Union force under General Benjamin F. Butler. But as Grant moved toward Cold Harbor, Aleck was ordered across the James to join the main army. In the fighting at Cold Harbor, Aleck and his horse were hit by seven rifle balls. One cut a lens of his field glasses, another broke a ring from his sword, a third hit him in the body, while others struck either his mount or his clothes.

With five other wounded officers, Aleck made the journey by wagon and train to Richmond. There he received from the Dudleys and the Gibsons the same loving care that John had been given two years before. Although at first fears were held for his recovery, within ten days Aleck was back at full duty. His injury caused him, however, to miss assignment to the temporary command of McGowan's Brigade, a position for which both A. P. Hill and Lee recommended him, in lieu of McGowan who had been seriously wounded at Spotsylvania. But compensation came by the end of the month when he became Colonel Alexander Haskell, commander of the 7th South Carolina Cavalry Regiment.

General Grant's determination "to fight it out on this line" underwent a re-examination after the thirty days of sacrifice which followed the first exchange in the Wilderness. Suddenly he boldly transferred his army south of the unbridged James River with the purpose of moving on Richmond from the southeast, and by mid-June Union warriors surged against the defenses of Petersburg. This maneuver surprised Lee, but he received important assistance from a series of makeshift defensive actions by the troops under Beauregard and soon the two armies found themselves locked in siege combat.

Lee's lines extended for miles, from the Chickahominy about Richmond across the James below Chaffin's Bluff and along the outskirts of Petersburg to a short distance north of Hatcher's Run. As the Federals put pressure on one flank and then the other, Lee's problem became how best to use his dwindling strength to oppose them. He moved troops from one side of the James River to the other as necessity required, and thus the action of October 7, 1864, on the Darbytown Road, southeast of Richmond, found both John and Aleck engaged.

The section of John's memoirs dealing with this fight is missing, so virtually all we know of his participation is that he narrowly escaped death when a Minié ball grazed his head. But Aleck wrote a full account of the engagement in his narrative of his war experiences. In the fighting he received a serious wound which destroyed his left eye. He again received the devoted attention of friends in Richmond and then went with his mother and father to his home in South Carolina to recuperate. So remarkable were his powers of recovery that despite the severity of his injury, he was back with his troops by the end of January 1865.

Joe and John were nearby and well. Joe by then was a captain and still on the staff of E. P. Alexander, who had reached the rank of brigadier general the previous spring. John, too, had received a promotion to lieutenant colonel, and the fourth of the brothers, Langdon, was shortly to transfer from his staff duties with McGowan's Brigade to a new assignment at division headquarters under General R. H. Anderson.

Before Aleck left home for Virginia, the seventh of the brothers, Lewis, enlisted, and the veteran of the Army of Northern Virginia helped the young recruit, who was nearing his eighteenth birthday, plan his journey to Virginia. "Lewis, like his brothers before him, is a soldier before he enters the field," Alexander wrote home. "I am sure of his success and his usefulness."

But Lewis reached Virginia only in time to view the rapid distintegration of the Confederacy, a process John describes so vividly in his memoirs. Aleck recalled the experience as "like a dream—moving, fighting, starving." At Appomattox, he was designated by General Lee to lead the cavalry, as John was the artillery, to the place where they turned their equipment over to the Federals.

Then the two ranking Haskells moved on to meet their brothers, Langdon, Joseph, and Lewis, and—their full obligation accomplished—the five turned their horses on the path to Abbeville and the quiet peace of "The Home Place." William and Charles were with so many of their comrades in eternal rest.

Notes

━━━━━━━━━━━〜〜〜━━━━━━━━━

Chapter 1.

1. South Carolina College, established in 1801, became the University of South Carolina in 1866. It was and is located at Columbia, the capital of the state.

2. The South Carolina Secession Convention met in Columbia December 17, 1860, but adjourned that day to meet in Charleston, because of an epidemic of smallpox in Columbia. On the next day at 4 P.M., the Convention reassembled in Institute Hall at Charleston amidst great excitement. The speaker's gavel displayed the word "Secession," engraved in "deep, black characters," and a crowd which wore blue cockades in hats and displayed a variety of flags, among which was none of the United States, moved noisily through the halls and up and down the stairs. To assist the speakers, whom the noise drowned out, the Convention moved again, this time to St. Andrew's Hall. Two days later, December 20, word spread through Charleston that the Ordinance of Secession would be presented and passed when the Convention assembled at noon. Business stopped and everyone who could went to the hall. When the Ordinance passed without a dissenting vote, the crowd cheered madly. The news passed quickly through the city that South Carolina no longer owed allegiance to the Yankee Nation but was independent. Even darkness had no effect upon the enthusiasm, for houses were brilliantly illuminated, and the night sky echoed

the music of numbers of bands. People carried home with them pieces of the palmetto trees which had stood on either side of the speaker's stand in St. Andrew's Hall, to be treasured as mementos of so memorable a day.

3. James M. Perrin was a prominent lawyer of Abbeville. Although he later became a colonel of his regiment, the term as used by Haskell here was the honorary one extended to Southern lawyers. He had served in the Mexican War, but his rank was that of lieutenant. He raised the company for Gregg's Regiment, with which he served as captain, major, lieutenant colonel, and colonel, the rank he held when he was killed at Chancellorsville, May 3, 1863.

4. Maxcy Gregg, a graduate of South Carolina and a practicing lawyer, had served in the Mexican War without seeing action. He was an ardent supporter of Southern rights and participated in the Secession Convention. When South Carolina seceded he became colonel of the First South Carolina Volunteers, and was in the action against Ft. Sumter, after which he took his regiment to Virginia. He was wounded slightly at First Manassas, and died in action at Fredericksburg. As a soldier he won praise from his commanders; A. P. Hill called him the "invincible pillar of my strength." But his personal interest lay in the classics, particularly Greek literature and philosophy, and in astronomy, for the study of which he had a private observatory in his home at Columbia.

5. Morris Island lies slightly south of the entrance to Charleston Harbor.

6. Sullivan's Island lies slightly to the north of the entrance to Charleston Harbor.

7. Nathan G. Evans, West Point '48, was known as "Shanks" to his comrades because of his knock-knees. Called a "riproaring, scorning-all-care type" of soldier by Fitzhugh Lee, Evans gained early military experience fighting Indians in the West. Before Sumter he acted as adjutant of the South Carolina forces, but reached Virginia in time to participate in First Manassas, where he correctly interpreted McDowell's flank attack, which he held up successfully against great odds until the Confederates could bring together other troops to withstand it.

8. Richard H. Anderson, West Point '42, won sufficient recognition in the Mexican War for his native state, South Carolina, to award him a sword. He resigned from the United States Army and entered the

South Carolina service on the secession of the state. After Sumter and a short tour of duty in Pensacola with Bragg, he was with the Army in Virginia for the remainder of the war, serving with Longstreet, McLaws and D. H. Hill, all of whom had been his classmates at West Point. Tall and muscular in appearance, he was, Mrs. Chesnut said, "the most silent and discreet of men." As a military leader, he won the affection of his associates and men, but his natural disinclination for effort—his "laziness," as some of his contemporaries called it—militated against him except when he was under the driving force of his good friend Longstreet.

9. Bee, a Charlestonian by birth, moved as a boy to Texas, where his father was secretary of state of the newly organized Republic of Texas. Strangely, in view of that seeming expatriation, Bee received an appointment as a "cadet at large" to West Point in 1841, and graduated four years later. He resigned from the United States Army March 3, 1861, and joined the South Carolina troops. He became a brigadier general of Confederate forces June 17, 1861, and joined the army of J. E. Johnston in the Shenandoah Valley. In First Manassas, his position on the Confederate left brought him into the severest fighting. Despite his green troops, he did excellent work in opposing the Federal flanking movement, although eventually the command was beaten back in a disorganized condition. Bee's death from wounds received in the battle made him a popular hero, while many of his contemporaries thought his ability of so high an order that they considered his early death a great loss to the Southern cause.

10. John Dunovant, son of R. G. M. Dunovant, who became adjutant general of the South Carolina forces after the state's secession, served in South Carolina until ordered to Virginia in March 1864. There his record was so noticeable that at the recommendation of President Davis he became a brigadier general. In a cavalry action on Vaughan Road, October 1, 1864, he persuaded his division commander to allow him to charge with his brigade. In the charge which accomplished its purpose of driving the enemy, Dunovant was killed.

11. Langdon Cheves, 1776–1857, was a member of Congress from Georgia and speaker of the House of Representatives in the 13th Congress, 1814–1815. He was president of the Bank of the United States, 1819–1822.

12. Haskell's brothers, Alexander and William, went to Virginia with the first troops from South Carolina, April 20, 1861.

13. According to the "Company Muster-in Roll" on file in the National Archives, Haskell on May 18, 1861, was a second lieutenant with Capt. W. R. Calhoun's company, First Regiment South Carolina Infantry. A note on the roll states, "This company subsequently became Company A, 1st Regiment South Carolina Artillery," organized March 25, 1862, but before that Company A was a part of the 1st Battalion South Carolina Artillery, "which was mustered into the service of the Confederate States in May, 1861, under the same enlistment."

14. William Ransom Calhoun was a South Carolinian who had been educated abroad and at West Point. He resigned from the army within a year of his graduation in 1850 to become a planter in his native state. His enthusiasm for the Southern cause took him into the service of the Confederacy where his career was marked with personal controversy. A difficulty over camping grounds with a Maryland regiment caused Mrs. Chesnut to term Calhoun and some associates "foolish, rash, hairbrained lads." Later he was arrested for writing an insulting letter about a commander, and a duel in September 1862 brought an end to his tempestuous life. At his death he was colonel of the First South Carolina Artillery Regiment.

15. Francis S. Bartow, who as mayor of Savannah agitated strenuously for the secession of Georgia, was a member of the Confederate Provisional Congress as well as regimental and brigade commander in the army. He was killed at First Manassas, and with Bee was eulogized as an early Southern hero. A shaft to his memory was shortly erected at the spot where he fell.

16. Johnston was then in command of what was called the Department of Northern Virginia, with his headquarters at Centerville, Virginia, between Manassas and Washington.

17. Gustavus W. Smith, a Kentuckian, West Point 1842, was Street Commissioner of New York City and prominent in Democratic politics when, with war imminent, he traveled South because of ill-health and his determination to join the Confederacy. In the United States Army, he never held rank above that of captain and resigned in 1854 to become a professional civil engineer. Much was expected of him as a Confederate officer, but ill health plagued him until his

resignation in early 1863. He served as a volunteer aide to Beauregard for a time, and then became the manager of a Georgia iron foundry and mining company. When Sherman started his campaign of 1864 in Georgia, Smith accepted a Georgia militia command, and was active in the latter phases of the Dalton-Atlanta campaign.

18. Haskell's service record shows an appointment as major, Commissary Department, with General G. W. Smith, effective December 21, 1861.

19. Horace Randal, West Point 1854, was a native of Tennessee but a resident of Texas. That may have been the reason why, after serving less than a year in the Virginia theater as a Confederate officer, he transferred to the Trans-Mississippi area.

20. Pierre G. T. Beauregard, a Louisianian of French extraction, graduated from West Point in 1838, and after more than two decades of service as an engineer officer returned to the Point as superintendent in 1860. His open avowal of Southern allegiance, however, caused his transfer within five days, and two months later, February 20, 1861, he resigned from the service. He was swept into a hero's role at Sumter and First Manassas, but from 1861 on he played a less prominent part until, in mid-1864, he correctly interpreted Grant's move to Petersburg. Typically French in appearance and soldierly in manner, he was fertile with plans which were almost universally unacceptable to the Richmond authorities.

21. James Ewell Brown Stuart earned the ironic nickname of Beauty at West Point, where he graduated in 1854. He was flamboyant and venturesome, traits which at times led him astray from the line of strict duty. But none of his boyish enthusiasms, which included a love of romantic folk music, blinded his ability for important military observation. He was innately religious but personally combative. His wife was the daughter of the Federal cavalry leader, Philip St. George Cooke, who more than once led his troops in combat against those of his son-in-law. Stuart, because of his initials, was popularly known among the Confederates as "Jeb," a name which moderns have accepted.

22. After First Manassas the Confederate army in Northern Virginia had a loose and at times confused organization under Johnston with Beauregard as an assistant. On October 21, 1861, the War Department ordered a general reorganization, and established the Department of Northern Virginia, with Johnston in command.

23. Johnston was born in 1807, which made him 54 in 1861.

24. George B. McClellan, West Point '46, was scholarly in his interests and was responsible for the adaptation of many features of the European armies to American use. In the old army days before the war, he and a group of friends, including J. E. Johnston, who called McClellan "Beloved Mac" in his letters, and G. W. Smith, planned some sort of filibustering expedition in Mexico, but nothing came of it.

  McClellan had had virtually no battle experience with troops when in 1861 he engaged in the campaign in West Virginia, the satisfactory results of which brought him the most important field command of the Federal army. An excellent organizer of an army, he proved less successful in the field, a failure attributable in part to the faulty intelligence he received from Allan Pinkerton, who greatly overestimated Confederate numbers.

25. The difficulty between Davis and Johnston, which had unfortunate results for the Confederacy, had more facets than Davis's efforts to direct from Richmond the tactical arrangements of Johnston's army. They had basic strategical differences. Where Davis dispersed troops, Johnston urged their concentration. Johnston insisted that a strategic retreat was better than a futile fight or a hopeless siege, a principle with which Davis was in fundamental disagreement.

  These differences were accentuated by the personal antagonism which for some reason existed between the two. It first reached public attention when Johnston objected in September 1861 to the ranking of the full generals of the Confederacy. Under the terms of the legislative act establishing the rank, Johnston as the ranking officer among them in the United States Army should have been first in the list of full generals. Instead, he was placed fourth, behind Cooper, A. S. Johnston and Lee. But Mrs. Johnston, in a letter which she wrote a friend in the summer of 1863, made it evident that the difference was of longer standing than the dispute over rank. In it she said that she had attempted to persuade her husband not to take service with the Confederacy, where he would be under Davis: "... he hates you, he has power and he will ruin you," she told her friend she had said to Johnston. But he ignored her advice and attempted as best he could to serve under Davis to the end.

26. Haskell evidences here a popular misconception which was based on Davis's argument after the event. In a conference with Beauregard and Johnston the night of First Manassas, Davis agreed that

no follow-up of the victory should be attempted. Later, he argued that he had no responsibility for the failure to pursue the defeated Federals.

27. John Gibbon, although Pennsylvania-born, was appointed to West Point from North Carolina, and had three brothers in the Confederate service. An artillery officer—he prepared the artillerists' manual for the Federal army—he proved a capable brigade, division and corps commander. At Appomattox, Gibbon was in command of the 24th Corps, and was one of the commissioners who arranged the details of the surrender of Lee's army. After the war, as a colonel of infantry, he engaged in much Indian fighting. As a part of that duty, he rescued the portion of Custer's command which was not engaged at Little Big Horn and buried the dead in that engagement.

Chapter 2.

1. Smith was not the first to hold the rank of major general in the Confederate army, as Twigg, Polk and Bragg all received it before him, and Van Dorn at the same time. But he was apparently the first major general in Johnston's army.

2. Davis made Beauregard a full general on the field of Manassas the morning after the battle.

3. The Battle of Seven Pines-Fair Oaks occurred May 31, 1862. Johnston was wounded late in the afternoon. Smith had little part in the engagement because of his illness, although his troops participated in it. As second to Johnston he succeeded to the command, but relinquished it after the next day's unimportant fighting. His second stroke was on the evening of June 2. Except for a brief period of unsuccessful field command in Northwestern Virginia from July to October, 1861, Lee's previous service for the Southern army had been in staff positions and in the supervision of coastal defenses in South Carolina and Georgia.

4. John B. Hood, a popular blond giant who became a Texan when his native Kentucky failed to secede, earned a reputation as a fighter while leading a brigade and division with the Army of Northern Virginia. He incurred a crippled arm at Gettysburg and a little more than two months later lost a leg at Chickamauga. His magnetic personality won the friendship of Jefferson Davis while he was in Richmond recuperating from his wounds. An excellent

leader of men, he was likely to be rash in attack. One story containing this implication was told by a Federal scout, who reported to Sherman, "I seed Hood bet $2,500 with nary a pair in his hand." He was misplaced when Davis supplanted Johnston with him in command of the Army of Tennessee in July 1864. He first met defeat by Sherman in the series of engagements about Atlanta between July and September, and Thomas then virtually destroyed his army before Nashville in December of that year. From then on Hood was without comand.

5. Writing as he was, largely from memory, Haskell is wrong about the commissioning of Randal as a brigadier general. He did command a brigade, almost from the time of his arrival in Texas, along toward the last of the summer of 1862, but it was as a colonel. Not until April 1864 was he made a brigadier, but he was killed that same month in the engagement at Jenkin's Ferry, Arkansas, so the promotion was never confirmed. But if Haskell was wrong about the time of the commission and of Randal's death, he was right about Randal's ability. Not only did Davis and Johnston appreciate him, but General "Dick" Taylor said after the battle at Mansfield, Louisiana, also of April 1864, "In vigor, energy and daring, Randal surpassed my expectations, high as they were. . . ."

6. The Battle of Leesburg (Ball's Bluff), fought October 21, 1861, was actually a skirmish between Federals, who crossed the Potomac without making adequate preparations for their retreat in the event one was necessary, and Confederates in an advanced position. Had it come later in the war it would hardly have earned more than the barest mention, but at the time it created much excitement with the Federals' preferring charges against their commander while the Confederates engaged in controversy as to who did what and when.

7. E. R. Burt, commander of the 18th Mississippi Infantry, was mortally wounded at Leesburg.

8. Tennent Lomax, who commanded the 3rd Alabama Infantry, was killed the next spring in the Battle of Seven Pines.

9. Eppa Hunton, who commanded the 8th Virginia Infantry at Leesburg, was a member of the Virginia Secession Convention. His advocacy of secession there was as a means of forcing a compromise and thus of averting otherwise inevitable war. When that effort failed he joined the military effort of the state and the Confederacy.

He was of striking appearance and was energetic in battle, but he frequently suffered ill health. He moved to the battle at Leesburg in a spring wagon, as, having undergone a short time before several surgical operations, he was incapable of riding a horse. Nevertheless his conduct in the battle won the commendation of all observers. He was wounded at Gettysburg in Pickett's charge, and received promotion to a brigadier general a month later. After the war he represented Virginia in both Houses of the Congress. He was the only Southern member of the Commission which decided the election of 1876 in Hayes' favor, but he refused to sign the statement of conclusions.

10. The Crittenden family was typical of the division which occurred in many of the Border States. Senator John J. Crittenden was the author of the Crittenden Resolutions, which he drew up after Lincoln's election with the hope of ameliorating the differences between North and South. George B. Crittenden graduated from West Point in 1832—many years before Calhoun, whose friendship he must have held for other reasons than association at West Point. He did not pursue a military career, but resigned from the service in 1843. However, he quickly joined the Confederacy, and was shortly made a major general. His command was badly defeated in the Battle of Mill Springs, Kentucky, for which he was officially censured. He resigned his commission and served thereafter as a volunteer aide to General J. J. Williams. His brother, Thomas L. Crittenden, entered the Federal service as a brigadier general in October 1861. After distinguished service at Shiloh, he received a promotion to major general, and participated in Murfreesboro and Chickamauga as a corps and wing commander. Rosencrans preferred charges against him after the Chickamauga defeat, but he was exonerated and served with the Army of the Potomac until his resignation, December 1864.

11. Jenifer's career offers interest for a number of reasons. He was not, apparently, a graduate of West Point, but was appointed a second lieutenant of dragoons in April 1847. When he resigned from the United States Army in March 1861, he was a first lieutenant of cavalry. A Marylander, he joined the Confederate army with the rank of captain of cavalry, but held the provisional rank of colonel. On September 24, 1861, he received command of the 8th Virginia Cavalry, and was with this regiment in southwest Virginia in the late spring of 1862, where for a time he commanded a brigade, but

still as a colonel. He was bitterly criticized for a retreat he ordered at Giles Court House in May 1862, and this may have been responsible for his failure to be re-elected in the reorganization of his regiment, a statement which appears on his service record. In August 1863, he commanded a post with a small body of troops at Selma, Alabama, but in December of that year is given as commanding a brigade with the Department of the Gulf, under General Dabney Maury. A year later, however, Maury refers to Jenifer in a dispatch as a captain, and in September 1864 Jenifer was assigned to the Andersonville prison as a captain of the provisional army. There is no notation on his service record or in the *Official Records* to explain this reduction in rank or change of service.

12. Apparently Haskell, Randal and the others kept this matter sufficiently quiet for it to have no effect upon the reputation of Evans, but trouble mounted in 1863 for this rough and ready soldier. He was tried in the early part of that year for both drunkenness and disobedience of orders. He was acquitted of both charges, but Beauregard, under whom he then served, considered him incompetent and removed him from command. His return to duty in the spring of 1864 was marred by serious injury through a fall from his horse, and he saw no further service until the next year.

13. Joseph Lane, a North Carolinian by birth, had a colorful career, which included life as a flatboat operator on the Mississippi and as superintendent of an Indian reservation. President Polk appointed him Territorial Governor of Oregon after an active participation in Indiana politics, but he gave up the position to become Territorial Representative to Congresss. When Oregon became a state, he was elected to the Senate, but did not stand for re-election because of his nomination for the Vice-Presidency. His open advocacy of secession led to all sorts of rumors, one that he planned a Pacific republic to include parts of Oregon and California as an ally of the Confederacy. Actually he lived quietly in his adopted state, with his political career a sacrifice to his pro-Southern sympathies.

14. John C. Breckinridge originally opposed secession, saying: "I am an American citizen, a Kentuckian, who never did an act nor cherished a thought that was not full of devotion to the Constitution and the Union." He presided over the Senate as Vice-President in the Buchanan administration until the inauguration of Lincoln, and then accepted election as Senator in the new Congress, taking his seat when the Senate met in the special session of July 1861. He

held strongly to the neutral position which he attributed to his state, and opposed all Lincoln's war measures. But when the Union forces occupied Kentucky in September 1861, he moved to the South. As a result the Senate expelled him as a traitor, for he was already active in the Confederate army. His service began as a brigadier general, although he was without military experience. He later became a major general, and in February 1865 he succeeded Seddon as Confederate Secretary of War.

15. It was Washington who, carrying a message from Johnston to Longstreet at the Battle of Seven Pines, rode into the Union lines and alerted the Federals to the impending Confederate attack.

16. Wade Hampton, Jr., served with Johnston's staff in Virginia and in the West, where Johnston went in December 1862, until the removal of Johnston as commander of the Army of Tennessee before Atlanta in July 1864. Hampton then transferred to his father's staff in Virginia. After the war, Haskell married his sister.

17. Lucius Q. C. Lamar, a Georgian by birth, achieved prominence as a lawyer and politician in Mississippi. His military service was as lieutenant colonel of the the the 19th Mississippi, but in the summer and fall of 1861 he suffered from an illness which incapacitated him for the field. On November 22, 1861, he wrote his wife that he was leaving Richmond for Johnston's headquarters. "There is some ill feeling between the Potomac generals and the President," he told her. "I fear that Cousin James Longstreet is taking sides against the administration. He will certainly commit a grave error if he does." Lamar was a consistent defender of Jefferson Davis, both during and after the war. His postwar career was among the most distinguished of ex-Confederates. He was a United States Senator from 1877 to 1885, when he became Secretary of the Interior in Cleveland's Cabinet. In 1887 he received an appointment to the United States Supreme Court, where he served until his death in 1893.

18. Lamar's illness is said by his biographer, W. A. Cate, to have been an "apoplectic attack," while Lamar himself described it in a letter to his wife as "slight rushes of blood to the head."

19. The plague of illnesses which troubled the army was especially noticeable among the recruits, who suffered from poorly prepared food, the sultry Virginia weather, and the contagious diseases, to which many of the rurally reared soldiers had not previously been

exposed. "They had almost everything," John B. Gordon wrote, "except teething, nettle-rash, and whooping-cough. I rather think some of them were afflicted with the latter disease."

20. The fight at Dranesville occurred December 20, 1861, when two foraging parties ran together.

21. "Old Peter," as the tenacious, dependable Longstreet was popularly called, was a West Point graduate of 1842, who served as a paymaster in the United States army before his resignation. Despite his lack of field experience with troops, he was made a brigadier general in the Confederate service on June 17, 1861, and from the beginning stood high in the regard of such army commanders as J. E. Johnston and Lee. He was a leader who had remarkable control of his emotions. A skillful poker player, he had no inclination to gamble in battle, but calculated carefully the chances of success, often being termed slow because of his deliberateness. Without the colorful qualities of some of his more dramatic comrades, Longstreet impressed observers by his calmness and lack of fear. Fitzhugh Lee noticed all this as early as First Manassas, and remarked of it again at Appomattox, ". . . the night before the surrender . . . , there was still the bulldog tenacity, the old genuine *sang froid* about him which made all feel he could be depended on to hold fast to his position as long as there was ground to stand on."

22. Charles W. Field of Kentucky was a classmate of Longstreet at West Point. He entered the Confederate service as a cavalryman, a subordinate of Stuart, whose commander he had been in the United States Army. Field transferred to the infantry in 1862 and made a sufficiently good record for Davis to give him the command of Hood's old division. But Longstreet wanted that assignment for Jenkins and asked why it went to Field. This angered Davis, who inspired the War Department to write Longstreet a letter in which the commander of Lee's First Corps was told that he was "highly insubordinate" and had earned rebuke. Field received the appointment and served capably to the surrender. After the war, Field was in the Egyptian army for a while, and upon his return to the United States held various positions with the Federal government, something of a paradox inasmuch as he was ineligible for the service—the army—for which the government had educated him.

23. Peyton T. Manning, chief of ordnance for Longstreet, had a strangely frightening experience at Chickamauga, where on the second day—September 20, 1863—several of the staff had gathered with their commander as the fighting continued to enjoy the unusual delicacy of a luncheon of Nassau bacon and Georgia sweet potatoes. As they were eating, a shell fragment struck Manning, who, in Longstreet's words, fell, "gasping, as was supposed, in the struggles of death." The others jumped to help him but to their surprise they discovered that he had just taken a large bite of sweet potato as the piece of shell hit him, and had choked on it. When he at last got the mouthful down, all were relieved to find that he had received but a slight wound.

24. ˈBeverley Johnston practiced law at the family home, Abingdon, Virginia.

25. Fauntleroy, whose rank in the Navy was that of lieutenant, resumed that service in November 1861, when he sailed with C.S.S. *Nashville* for Great Britain.

26. Known to his close friends as Powell, A. P. Hill, West Point '47, suffered through the war from ill health. Quick to sense what he considered an injustice, he clashed with both Jackson and Longstreet over official matters, coming close to a duel with Longstreet. In all instances Lee used his ameliorating influence to smooth things over. A good fighter, Hill was not consistent, but he impressed himself sufficiently on Jackson and Lee for both men, when on their deathbeds, to recall him above all their associates. Hill's death occurred on April 2, 1865, the day after he returned to duty from a fit of illness. The situation that morning was one of grave danger for the Confederates, who had suffered defeat the day before at Five Forks and were to start that night the retreat to Appomattox. Hill was riding with an orderly when they encountered a group of Federal soldiers. Without hesitation Hill demanded their surrender, but their response was the fire which wounded him mortally.

27. Robert A. Toombs was an aggressive leader in the organization of the Confederate government and served as the first Secretary of State in Davis's Cabinet. In July 1861 he became a brigadier general in the army and immediately engaged in controversies with his superiors over the failure to initiate an offensive campaign. He resigned after Sharpsburg, but his bombastic attitude, temper, and hatred of Davis kept him in constant controversy until the end of the war.

28. Lucius J. Gartrell, a Georgian, had studied law in Toombs's office
before the war. He entered politics and was a member of Congress
from 1857 until with the others of the Georgia delegation he withdrew upon the secession of their state in 1861. He organized the 7th
Georgia, became its colonel, and received the commendation of
Johnston for his conduct in the Battle of First Manassas. He left the
army when he was elected to the Confederate Congress, but at the
expiration of his term re-entered the military service as a brigadier
general, and served in that rank until wounded near the end of the
war.

29. Richard Ewell, West Point '40, an eccentric himself, as Haskell
says, suspected Jackson's sanity when Stonewall said that he
couldn't use salt as it affected his left leg. An important subordinate
of Jackson, Ewell would slip about on reaching the front areas to
avoid Jackson's knowing he was there. He lost a leg at Second
Manassas and married shortly after, with the result that Randolph
McKim said of him, Ewell afterwards "was not the same soldier he
had been when he was a whole man—and a single man." Known as
"Old Baldhead," Ewell once explained the contrast between his
heavy beard and his lack of hair, that it must be because he used
his brains more than he did his jaws.

30. Jubal A. Early graduated from West Point in '37 but resigned a
year later to enter the practice of law. He was inclined to take up
causes, popular or unpopular. He opposed secession as a member
of Virginia's convention, but immediately entered the Southern
army, once the decision was made. Irascible and with a bitter
tongue at times, Early, in the words of Robert Stiles, "was in
some respects a bundle of inconsistencies and contradictions of
religion and irreligion; of reverence and profanity." Early and
Beauregard supervised the drawings in the Louisiana Lottery, to
the disgust of many of their former comrades, at a salary variously
estimated from $12,000 to $30,000 a year. One periodical writer
of the time, after watching one of the drawings, said this: "General Early is over six feet tall; he still affects gray cloth, and, with
his patriarchal beard and stoop, certainly has a saintly look as he
sits on the platform and calls off 'fortune's favorites.' He makes no
claim to saintliness, however, and it is well known that when he
was the trusted lieutenant of Lee and was fighting up and down
the Valley with limited resources, 'Old Jube' could hold his own
with any mule-driver in the Confederacy."

31. Isaac R. Trimble, a Kentuckian by birth but a Marylander by adoption, graduated from West Point in 1822. Ten years later he resigned to engage as a professional engineer in the expanding construction of railroads throughout the country. When war began he is said to have burned a number of railroad bridges in the Baltimore-Washington area, and thus incurred the extreme displeasure of the Federal authorities. Trimble lost a leg leading his men on the last day of Gettysburg, and was captured. But Secretary of War Stanton warned that he should not be paroled or allowed communication with anyone as a "dangerous man." He was not exchanged until just a few weeks before the end of the war. Trimble achieved the rank of major general, the highest held by any Marylander in the Confederate army.

32. Thomas J. Jackson, West Point '46, resigned from the United States Army in 1852 because of his conviction that barracks life would destroy initiative. He joined the faculty of Virginia Military Institute, where he was teaching when he entered the Confederate service. After spending some time training troops, Jackson received an assignment to Harper's Ferry, where he entered an interesting negotiation with the Baltimore and Ohio. The railroad agreed to pass all its trains through Harper's Ferry between the hours of noon and 1 P.M. As soon as the agreement was operative, Jackson placed troops about twenty miles apart, to block the passage of trains. By so doing he caught and captured a large part of the rolling stock of the B. & O., and sent it south to add to the Confederacy's resources. Shortly after, he was superseded by General J. E. Johnston, in whose army he commanded a regiment, then a brigade and after the army's reorganization a division.

The major reorganization of the army occurred October 22, 1861, with the creation of the Department of Northern Virginia under Joseph E. Johnston. Three subordinate districts were established: the Potomac under Beauregard, until he left for the West in January 1862; Acquia under T. H. Holmes; Shenandoah Valley under Jackson. G. W. Smith, Longstreet and Kirby Smith were division commanders in the District of the Potomac. Haskell is wrong about Huger, who commanded at Norfolk and was not a part of Johnston's department.

33. Theophilus H. Holmes, a North Carolinian, was a classmate of Jefferson Davis at West Point, where the two men began a close friendship which lasted after their graduation. When Holmes en-

tered the Confederate service, Davis promptly commissioned him a brigadier general. In the Battles of the Seven Days, Holmes made less than a brilliant record as a division commander, but was promoted to lieutenant general and given command of the Trans-Mississippi Department. At his own request, in early 1863 he was relieved of the department command but again failed as a field commander, and ended the war in charge of the North Carolina militia.

34. Benjamin Huger, like Holmes, was one of the older active commanders of the Confederacy, having graduated from West Point in 1825. He had the misfortune to become involved in controversy over his conduct in the engagement of Seven Pines-Fair Oaks, where Longstreet threw an undeserved onus on him, and he failed in the Seven Days to cut off McClellan's retreat after Malvern Hill. After that he served in the Trans-Mississippi Department as an inspector of ordnance.

35. Edmund Kirby Smith had a reputation for being easygoing among his classmates at West Point, where he graduated in 1845, but some indication of the reverse is shown by his rising to become a major of cavalry within 16 years. After serving in Virginia, Kirby Smith went first to East Tennessee and then to the Trans-Mississippi, where he succeeded Holmes in command. At his death, Kirby Smith was the last surviving full general of the Confederacy.

36. Joseph Sweeney was a minstrel who "jined the cavalry" to the great pleasure of Jeb Stuart. Wherever Stuart was, Sweeney was close by, with gay songs or appealing hymns to suit the mood of his commander. When in camp, where young ladies could join the fun, Sweeney played lively dance tunes on his banjo. He rode to legendary fame with Stuart.

37. Although Jackson was appointed to the rank of brigadier general as of June 17, 1861, it was not confirmed by the Senate until August 28. As early as July, however, Lee refers to him in an order as Brigadier General Jackson, and in the orders issued July 20 for the fighting at First Manassas, Jackson is called a brigadier general, in which rank he signed his report of July 23 about that engagement. It is obvious that Haskell is in error about Johnston's having sent him to "Colonel" Jackson, as Haskell was not in Virginia until after First Manassas. It is possible that Jackson could have been wearing a captured blue uniform with the Federal

insignia for a colonel, an eagle (the Confederate insignia for the rank was three stars in line on the collar), as that was not uncommon then. But Jackson, the following May, in the midst of his remarkable Valley Campaign, issued an order against any of his men wearing Federal uniforms. Just how to resolve all this, one hesitates to say. It is possible that Haskell confused in his memory of the incident Jackson's rank because he was wearing the Federal uniform he describes.

38. Nathan Bedford Forrest, the remarkable cavalry leader of the western theater, won renown, which he continues to hold, by his spectacular achievements. He had an instinctive understanding of military tactics, although without training or previous experience. He never held important, independent command, nor did he ever have a large body of troops, but he performed with striking success under those handicaps. There is a story, told by F. L. Riley in *General Robert E. Lee after Appomattox* but considered apocryphal by some authorities, that General Lee told the British military leader Viscount Wolseley that Forrest was the most capable of his subordinates: "He accomplished more with fewer troops than any other officer on either side." Whether true or not—Dabney Maury attributes something of the same opinion to J. E. Johnston—the story expresses the conviction of many Confederate soldiers.

39. Richard Taylor was the only son of Zachary Taylor and the brother of Jefferson Davis's first wife. His early life was spent in frontier army posts, but he was educated in Europe, at Harvard, and at Yale, where he graduated. A sugar planter in Louisiana, he entered Confederate service early, and took part in both Jackson's campaign in the Shenandoah Valley and in the Seven Days below Richmond. He then went to the western theater, where he ended the war as commander of the department which included the area from Georgia to Louisiana.

40. The battle of Fredericksburg occurred December 13, 1862.

41. Thomas G. Rhett of South Carolina, West Point '45, joined Johnston's staff just in time to be given the responsibility of hastening arriving troops and ammunition to the battlefield of Manassas, a task he performed so well that he received the praise of the commander in the latter's official report. After the Peninsula campaign, Rhett, who never rose higher than major, transferred to the Trans-Mississippi Department.

42. William H. C. Whiting, West Point '45, received promotion to a brigadier general for his work as an engineer officer for Johnston's Army of the Shenandoah at First Manassas, but Whiting had unequal success as a commander of troops and came into the disfavor of the President because he thought unwise Davis's plan to organize brigades and divisions exclusively with troops from the same state. Called "Little Billy" affectionately by his troops, Whiting transferred from the Army of Northern Virginia after 1862 and served in other theaters, usually as an engineer officer. He became a major general in 1863, and died a prisoner in May 1865 of wounds received at the fall of Fort Fisher, North Carolina, January 15.

43. James H. Hill, West Point '55, was severely wounded at First Manassas as a member of Bee's staff. After his recovery he served with Whiting as major and assistant adjutant general until his capture at the fall of Fort Fisher.

44. The circumstances of Jackson's acquiring his nickname are possibly as widely known as the Battle of First Manassas itself. R. M. Johnston in his *Bull Run: Its Strategy and Tactics* questions the authenticity of the story, which first appeared four days after the battle in the *Charleston Mercury*. Mrs. Chesnut, in an entry dated July 24, 1861, applied the name to Jackson's regiment, not to him, while on August 9, 1861, the *Richmond Whig and Advertiser* used Stonewall Brigade without application to the commander.

45. While his division was moving from the Shenandoah Valley to join the Army of Northern Virginia in late June 1862, Jackson rode ahead for a conference with Lee. He is said to have himself set the date of June 26 for the attack at Beaver Dam Creek or Mechanicsville. Whether from fatigue or the inability of his troops to move as fast as he expected, Jackson failed to reach his position by the appointed time. Late in the afternoon, A. P. Hill decided to initiate the battle without Jackson and opened the campaign of the Seven Days. Although at great cost, his troops hit the enemy with such intensity that in the night the Federals withdrew to Gaines's Mill. On the next day, with Jackson finally in place but principally because of Longstreet's attack, the Confederates drove the Federals from their second position.

46. Haskell refers to the mysterious failure of Jackson at White Oak Swamp, June 30, 1862, where he held his troops inactive and let

the opportunity escape to strike the Federals as they moved through the dense undergrowth of the swamp. The only logical explanation is that Jackson, who had little rest and sleep in the preceding week, was in virtually a stupor from fatigue.

47. Jackson's Valley campaign in the spring of 1862 is a remarkable example of a general's use of a small force to baffle completely his more numerous enemy. By the rapid marches which earned his soldiers the descriptive term "foot cavalry," as well as by the remarkable fighting spirit he instilled in them, Jackson drove the Federals from the Valley and frightened the Washington authorities to such a degree that they withheld McDowell's force from McClellan, and thus aided the Confederates in the defense of Richmond.

48. Chancellorsville, May 1–4, 1863, was a display of Lee and Jackson at their best. The Federals had a heavy advantage in numbers, as Longstreet with a major part of his corps was not with the Army of Northern Virginia. The plan of Hooker, the Federal commander, was to hold the attention of the Confederates with the troops on his left, while he moved those of his center and right to attack the rear and flank of the Southern army. But Lee and Jackson turned his tactics against him. Leaving the Confederates on the right to face the Federal left, Lee moved the rest of his army to face the approaching enemy. But then in an astounding move, he again divided his already outnumbered force and sent Jackson to strike the right rear of the Federals. The result was a crushing defeat for the bewildered Northerners, but a far greater calamity for the Southerners, who lost Jackson from a fatal wound received after nightfall, May 3, by the fire of his own men.

49. Second Manassas, August 23–30, 1862, is an excellent example of Lee's use of his team of Jackson and Longstreet to confuse and defeat the enemy. Pope, the bombastic Union commander who thought himself destined to succeed McClellan, was completely baffled by the rapid movements of Jackson, who got in the Federals' rear and captured their important supply base at Manassas. Pope turned to defeat Jackson, whom he assumed to be isolated, but Lee brought up Longstreet, and the Southern army gave its enemy a resounding whipping.

50. Haskell's opinions were formed in circumstances when loyalties made it difficult to attempt objective evaluations. A modern historian would hardly call Sherman a politician of any sort, in view of his open snub of Secretary of War Stanton, when the latter tried to shake his hand at the Grand Review of Sherman's troops in Washington after the close of the war. And Grant on the record was an adaptable, resourceful commander. In the Mississippi campaign, when it was necessary to cut his army loose from its sources of supply, he did so without hesitation, despite the prophecies of disaster. In Virginia, where Haskell saw him campaign, the situation demanded the exertion of power, and Grant used it without stint.

Chapter 3.

1. The commission is dated December 21, 1861.
2. Wade Hampton was a wealthy South Carolinian and one of the largest slaveowners of the South. Nevertheless, he opposed secession, but once South Carolina seceded, he committed himself without stint to the Southern cause. He raised Hampton's Legion, which contained infantry, cavalry and artillery, and purchased much of its equipment himself. Large in physique, he stood out dominantly in a group, while his experience as an outdoorsman contributed to his capabilities as a leader. Without previous military experience, he quickly adapted himself and rose steadily in the esteem of his superiors. Once he committed himself to the cavalry, his achievements made him second only to Stuart in that arm of the Confederate forces. Hampton's daughter, Sally, became Haskell's wife in June 1867.
3. Occoquan is a small village about 12 miles southeast of the battlefield of Manassas.
4. Major T. F. Fisher of Louisiana; later he transferred to the 6th Louisiana Infantry.
5. Dr. Edwin S. Gaillard and Dr. A. M. Fauntleroy. Dr. Fauntleroy was a Virginian and Dr. Gaillard a South Carolinian.
6. Hamilton, who does not appear in the index to the *Official Records,* or the *List of Staff Officers of the Confederate States Army 1861–1865,* or Estes: *Field Officers, Regiments, and Battalions in the Confederate States Army, 1861–1865,* apparently retired to civilian life before the end of the war. Mrs. Chesnut refers to him in March 1865 as Mr. Hamilton.
7. Dr. Gaillard served on the faculty also of the Virginia Medical College, and as editor at various times of the *Richmond Medical*

Journal, the *American Medical Weekly,* and *Gaillard's Medical Journal.* In 1863 he became general inspector of Confederate hospitals. Dr. Gibson, who had been professor of surgery at the Medical College of Richmond, served as surgeon general of the Virginia forces before the state entered the Confederacy. Mrs. Chesnut, who knew him well, called him the "very beau-ideal of a family physician."

8. Dr. J. W. Powell was surgeon of Gregg's First Regiment of South Carolina Volunteers before joining Hill.

9. This period was one of great administrative discord and difficulty for the Confederates. There were many bitter passages between the generals in the field and the War Department, as well as indignant protests by state authorities to the Administration in Richmond. In December 1861 the Congress passed the Bounty and Furlough Act, and in April 1862 the Conscription Act. The first was intended to encourage the re-enlistment of the men whose terms of service were about to expire. In re-enlisting, though, the men could choose any branch of service they wished. Many infantrymen consequently sought to leave that arduous branch for what they conceived as easier duty in the artillery or cavalry. Thus veterans of one branch became no better than recruits in another. Should they dislike for any reason the officers of the unit in which they were, they could leave it to re-enlist in another; or should enough of them dislike the officers they could refuse to re-elect, thus losing for the army the effective service of capable leaders who achieved unpopularity by being strict disciplinarians. The Conscription Act held the threat of enforced service over the head of men who prided themselves on their volunteer status, while it threatened to invade the rights of the states, which had granted exemption for a variety of reasons. The result of these legislative acts was great confusion, to which the Administration added by its insistence that units from companies through divisions should be composed of men from the same state.

10. As spring drew nearer in 1862, with its promise of renewed active campaigning, Johnston began to worry about his advanced position and McClellan's intentions. He was sure that he could not properly cover Richmond from his Manassas–Centerville line, should the enemy decide to move as he feared by the Potomac and Chesapeake Bay. At a conference with Davis February 20, Johnston

received orders to fall back to a position from which he could cover the capital under any eventuality. By the third week in March he had his army behind the Rapidan, where he was in the path should McClellan move overland, while he could counter quickly should the move be by water. McClellan chose the latter, and on April 2 his troops began to disembark at Fortress Monroe, at the foot of the Virginia Peninsula.

The Confederates had only a relatively small force in the area under the command of "Prince John" Magruder, who, however, fooled his enemy by marching and countermarching into believing he had a strong army. Although Johnston thought it unwise, as he considered the Peninsula a trap wherein the enemy could use either of the navigable rivers—the York and the James—to pass his flanks and land in his rear, the Confederate high command decided to oppose the Federals in the Peninsula. The army consequently moved to occupy the Yorktown–Warwick River line, which Magruder had prepared. Just as McClellan was ready to launch his attack, for which he had prepared with a tremendous weight of artillery, Johnston began a strategic retreat up the Peninsula. He fought a rearguard action at Williamsburg, May 5, in which neither army held a decided advantage, and by the middle of the month had his army in front of Richmond, where he awaited a blunder by the enemy, so that he might have a chance against their superior numbers.

11. David R. Jones, West Point '46, entered the Confederate service as a major, and as Beauregard's chief of staff carried the terms of surrender to Fort Sumter, April 13, 1861.

12. Raphael J. Moses, a Charlestonian by birth, after service as chief commissary with Longstreet's Corps, received assignment in 1864 as agent in Georgia for the subsistence department in Richmond. As such he was in Washington, Georgia, when Davis's party reached there on the flight from Richmond in May 1865. By official order Moses received $35,000 to $40,000—the amount varies in the different accounts—in silver bullion from the remains of the Confederate Treasury. It was to be used to purchase food for ill and needy Confederates, and Moses turned the amount over for that purpose to the Federal Provost General at Augusta, after which the money remains unaccounted for.

13. *The Wanderer,* which was built for a pleasure vessel, was purchased in 1859 by a Georgian, C. A. L. Lamar, who used it for

what is said to have been the last slave-running voyage to the South. Lamar and his crew took on 400 Negroes at Brazzaville on the Congo, and landed them on the coast of Georgia. Lamar and his associates were arrested and brought before the Federal courts. Some of the Negroes were seized by the United States Marshal for return to Africa, but others were sold and scattered over the South. While the matter was still in the courts, war started, and nothing was done; although in 1896 the marshal was reimbursed by Act of Congress for his expenses while searching for the Negroes.

14. The Battle of Seven Pines or Fair Oaks was fought May 31, 1862, when Johnston decided that McClellan had made the error for which the Confederates had waited. Two Federal corps were south of the Chickahominy, separated from the rest of the army by the river, swollen by flood, and the swamps of the area. Johnston had a simple plan, with Longstreet moving to hit the right flank of the Union forces while the rest of the Confederates attacked them in front. But Longstreet either misunderstood his orders or decided to change them, and marched to join the frontal assault. Although the weight of the Confederate attack drove the Federals back, Sumner by an unusual effort got his corps across the Chickahominy and secured a position which threatened the Southerners' left and rear. It was in an effort to defend against this that Johnston received the wound which incapacitated him for about five months and gave command of the Army of Northern Virginia to Lee.

15. Mechanicsville or Beaver Dam Creek, June 26, 1862, was the first of the battles of the Seven Days. (See note 45, Chapter 2.)

16. Turner Ashby, one of the South's fine amateur soldiers, gave promise of being among the most effective cavalry leaders of the Confederacy, but he died in a minor engagement of January 1862 in the Shenandoah Valley.

17. This was the Battle of Gaines's Mill or First Cold Harbor, fought June 27, 1862, in which A. P. Hill, Jackson and Longstreet combined to drive the Federals under Porter. Magruder's part in the engagement—a part he performed capably—was so to occupy the attention of the Union forces on the south side of the river that they would feel incapable of sending help to Porter. Gaines's Mill was the second engagement of the Seven Days.

18. John B. Magruder, West Point '30, was an eligible bachelor who won the attention of many of his associates by his ability as a

conversationalist, his fastidious dress and love of theatricals. Known as "Prince John," he was a great dissembler as when he used his small force early in the Peninsula campaign to create the illusion of large numbers by marching it back and forth, and in and out of clumps of forest. After the war he refused to accept parole and joined Maximilian in Mexico. At the end of Maximilian's career in Mexico, Magruder returned to the United States.

19. In his report of the Seven Days, Longstreet said: "Major Haskell, of General D. R. Jones' staff, volunteered his services to me for the day. Upon his first field, his conduct would have done credit to any distinguished veteran." This was but one of the commendations Haskell received for his participation in Gaines's Mill. He served that day under five generals: Longstreet, Jones, A. P. Hill, Magruder, and Whiting. All of them mentioned him in their reports.

20. George E. Pickett, a Virginian, owed his appointment to West Point to Abraham Lincoln, who—then a Congressman from Illinois —was a close friend of an uncle of Pickett's, and much of his advancement in the Confederate army to Longstreet. According to Sorrel, Longstreet's chief of staff, Pickett was "distinguished and striking" in appearance, particularly because of his hair, which in "long ringlets flowed loosely over his shoulders, trimmed and highly perfumed," while his beard was also curled and held the "scents of Araby." This commander, whose name is attached to the Confederates' supreme effort on the third day of Gettysburg, also attracted Sorrel's attention by the lengthy letters he wrote his sweetheart, later his wife, letters which she used as the basis of books in the postwar years.

21. Mrs. Chesnut lists "Braddy" Warwick among those for whom Sally Buchanan Campbell Preston had a fatal attraction. "Buck, the very sweetest woman I ever knew," said Mrs. Chesnut, "had a knack of being fallen in love with at sight, and of never being fallen out of love with. But there seemed a spell upon her lovers; so many were killed or died of the effects of wounds; Ransom Calhoun, Braddy Warwick, Claude Gibson, the Notts." *A Diary from Dixie,* ed. by Ben Ames Williams, Houghton, Mifflin Co., 280-281.

22. Christopher Columbus Upson was a native of New York, but was practicing law in Texas when the war began. At the time of the Seven Days he was a volunteer on Whiting's staff, but later in the year was made an associate justice of Arizona Territory by the Confederate government.

23. Charles S. Venable, a college teacher of mathematics and astronomy before and after the war, joined Lee's staff when the general in 1862 became military adviser to Davis. A major then, he became a colonel by the end of the war. Dignified and learned, he was also forceful yet temperate in manner. Possibly these qualities were responsible for his becoming the intercessor for the staff with Lee when the general, for whatever reason, was upset.

24. John T. Darby, according to Mrs. Chesnut, barely escaped lynching as a Southern spy in Philadelphia, where she said he remained too long as a faculty member of the medical college. And when he reached Atlanta, where he reported himself as from Philadelphia, he again had difficulty, as he was accused of being a Northern spy.

25. Thomas M. Logan, of South Carolina, became one of the most prominent railroad organizers after the war. At the time of which Haskell writes, Logan was a captain, but he rose through grades to become colonel of the legion and in February 1865 a brigadier general. Logan was with J. E. Johnston in April 1865 at the surrender to Sherman, who would hardly believe that so young a man could be in command of a brigade. Logan was born November 3, 1840, and was then but little more than 24 years old.

26. Dr. J. S. D'Orsay Cullen of Virginia.

27. Haskell must refer here to the ships of Alexander Collie and Company, not to Collie himself. This British firm of shipowners engaged in blockade-running as long as their vessels could make their way through the Federal blockade.

28. Theodore W. Hoenninger, whom the owners of the Spotswood brought from New York in 1861 to manage the hotel, is listed as a volunteer aide in Smith's report of the Battle of Seven Pines.

29. Thomas Underwood Dudley was one of Richmond's prominent merchants. His son, Thomas Underwood Dudley, Jr., after the war entered the Episcopal clergy. After nine years as Assistant Bishop, in 1884 he became Bishop of the Diocese of Kentucky.

30. Richard Hooker Wilmer of Virginia, a graduate of Yale and the Theological Seminary of Virginia, was elected Bishop of Alabama November 21, 1861, after the withdrawal of the Southern dioceses from the Protestant Episcopal Church in the United States. His election was accepted by the Southern church, acting autonomously, and he was consecrated at Richmond the following March.

A distinguished preacher, Bishop Wilmer received an honorary degree from Cambridge University, England, while attending the Lambeth Conference of 1867. In his later years, he wrote a book, *The Recent Past from a Southern Standpoint.* It contains virtually no historical detail.

31. In the fighting at Gaines's Mill John Haskell performed important staff duties for Generals Lee, Magruder, Longstreet, R. H. Anderson, D. R. Jones, and Whiting before he was wounded. Magruder in his report listed Haskell among those who had distinguished themselves in the action, as did his divisional commander, D. R. Jones. General Whiting paid him a high compliment in his report where he said: "Though not on my staff, I should not do right were I not to mention here the chivalrous daring of young Major Haskell of South Carolina, belonging, as I am told, to the staff of General D. R. Jones. His personal bearing in a most deadly fire, his example and directions, contributed not a little to the enthusiasm of the charge of the Third. I regret to say that the brave young officer received a terrible wound from a shell, but walked from the field as heroically as he had gone into the fire."

General Longstreet also paid Haskell a fine tribute in his report in which he stated: "Upon his first field, [Major Haskell's] conduct would have done credit to any distinguished veteran. After gallantly bearing the colors of one of the regiments to the enemy's breastworks and planting the standard upon them he lost his right arm by a cannonshot."

Chapter 4.

1. In the period of Haskell's recovery from his wound, the Army of Northern Virginia engaged in the rest of the Seven Days' fighting —Savage Station, Frayser's Farm, and Malvern Hill—the Second Bull Run campaign, and the invasion of Maryland with its climax at Sharpsburg or Antietam. Thus he missed some of the great days of Lee's army. Fredericksburg, which saw his return to service, was a futile effort by the Federals to dislodge the Confederates from their commanding position overlooking the town.

2. Joseph B. Kershaw, a South Carolina lawyer, made a good record as a regimental, brigade and division commander with Longstreet. Dignified and sincerely religious, he objected to Beauregard over the possible choice of "Bull Run" as the designation of the battle fought along that stream. Beauregard's reply did not tend to ease his disturbance: "Let us try and make it as great a name as your South Carolina Cowpens." But the Confederates did choose to call the battle by the name of the nearby railroad junction, Manassas, leaving Bull Run to the Federals.

3. Haskell, despite his modest denial of doing anything, received the praise of Longstreet for "important" service at Fredericksburg.

4. John G. Foster of New Hampshire, West Point '46, was at Sumter as an engineer officer, and his reports offer some of the best material available about conditions there under the attack of the Confederates. He was a capable, dependable commander, and in '64–'65, as a major general in charge of the Department of the South, co-operated effectively with Sherman in the campaigns against Savannah and Charleston.

5. Samuel G. French, West Point '43, was a native of New Jersey but became a Mississippi planter, when he resigned from the army in 1856, on properties his wife inherited. Upon the secession of Mississippi he joined the state's forces, and then went into the Confederate army, where his friendship with Jefferson Davis was an aid. He became a brigadier general in the fall of 1861 and a major general the next year. A difficulty with Longstreet in the late spring of 1863 caused French's transfer to the army in Mississippi under J. E. Johnston, who protested it to Richmond on the grounds that reports to him were that the troops resented so many generals of Northern birth. Davis defended French as a Mississippi resident, and Johnston accepted him. He served with Johnston again in the Atlanta campaign as a division commander of the Army of Tennessee and then with Hood through the defeat at Nashville, where the Federals virtually destroyed that army. French did not go to North Carolina with the remnant of that army.

6. G. W. Smith commanded the Department of North Carolina and Southern Virginia from its creation, September 19, 1862, until January 28, 1863, when French took temporary command. French had been a subordinate of Smith and resumed that position when D. H. Hill became the departmental commander on February 25. On the following day, Longstreet assumed command of the department, but on April 1, the department was reorganized, with Hill in command of the troops in North Carolina and French those in Southern Virginia. This was in preparation for the start

of the summer's campaigns, when Longstreet would return to his post as corps commander with the Army of Northern Virginia.

7. Daniel Harvey Hill, West Point '42, was a North Carolinian. A teacher of mathematics, he wrote a textbook on the subject and used the problems he included to ridicule Northerners and their business practices. Outspoken in his opinions and a good battle leader, Hill never quite made the most of his opportunities. Haskell is wrong in saying that Hill's appointment as a lieutenant general was a temporary one. There was a law for such a purpose and the appointment of Early, R. H. Anderson, A. P. Stewart and S. D. Lee as lieutenant generals were made under it. But Hill's appointment was not a temporary one. He was sent to join the Army of Tennessee in the summer of 1863 and the appointment was to fill a need in that army. But after the Battle of Chickamauga, when Bragg, then commanding the Army of Tennessee, allowed the fruits of the victory to escape him, Hill was a leader among the generals who insisted that the army should be given a new commander. Bragg was a favorite of Davis, who refused thereafter to send Hill's nomination to the Congress for confirmation as a permanent lieutenant general. Hill held no further active duty until the North Carolina campaign of Johnston against Sherman in 1865, after military control had been taken from Davis and assigned to Lee.

8. The campaign against New Bern was from March 8 to 16, 1863.

9. James Johnston Pettigrew earned his first distinction as an undergraduate at the University of North Carolina, and upheld his reputation in later life as a lawyer, writer and diplomat. Chosen as a colonel of a regiment at the outbreak of the war, he enlisted as a private when the regiment disbanded, but shortly received another colonelcy. He achieved praise from his associates for his skill as a tactical commander and his qualities of leadership. Despite this earned respect, Pettigrew at first declined promotion to brigadier general, but was prevailed upon to accept it. A slender, handsome man, Pettigrew was quick of decision and attractive in personality.

10. James L. Petigru preferred the shorter form of the family name. Called the "greatest private citizen South Carolina ever produced," it was also said of him that he was the only resident of the state who never seceded. His remark about wartime inflation was much

quoted: 'You take your money to market in your market basket and bring home your groceries in your pocketbook." Despite his opposition to secession and the war, the people of Charleston erected a monument to him after his death, March 9, 1863. In the inscription it bears they paid tribute to his courage in upholding the right as he saw it.

11. Matthew F. Maury was of Virginia birth, but lived his boyhood in Tennessee. Self-educated and an indefatigable worker, he became a professional naval officer and a distinguished oceanographer. He resigned April 20, 1861, from the United States Navy and soon received a commission as commander in the Confederacy. Modest and with the ruddy complexion of a sailor he made an ideal spokesman for the Confederacy in England, where his reputation and his appearance won favor.

12. Pettigrew was exchanged in August 1862. In his report of the expedition to New Bern, Pettigrew praised Haskell, saying that he "discharged his whole duty."

13. The seige of Washington which is on the Tar River just before it goes into the Pamlico River began March 30, 1863, and ended April 20, when the Confederates withdrew. Fort Hill was at Hill's Point, across the river and downstream from Washington.

14. Wharton J. Green, lieutenant colonel of the 2nd North Carolina battalion of infantry before becoming a staff officer, had less luck at Gettysburg, where he was severely wounded and then captured.

15. Junius C. Daniel, West Point '51, resigned from the army in 1858 and became a Louisiana planter, but on the outbreak of the war he returned to his native North Carolina, where he accepted the colonelcy of an infantry regiment. Promoted to a brigadier general in September 1862, Daniel led his brigade with such distinction that it earned the reputation of always advancing when ordered, and of never retreating unless directed to do so. Daniel died of wounds received at Spotsylvania, May 13, 1864.

16. Leventhorpe, who became a naturalized American citizen before the war, was a tall, handsome man who had been a British officer and was reputed to be the best-qualified field officer in the Confederate army. Wounded and captured at Gettysburg, he was held prisoner for nine months. After exchange he was offered a promotion to a brigadier general but refused it and then accepted

the same post with North Carolina state troops. He served in that capacity with Johnston's army in the last campaign in North Carolina.

17.   Haskell arrived at Culpeper Court House to join Longstreet June 8, 1863. Longstreet had been sent to the south side of the James in February with two of his divisions to protect Richmond against the reported arrival of a heavy body of Federal troops at Newport News. When no offensive move by the enemy against Richmond developed, Longstreet remained in the area supposedly to collect supplies from North Carolina and Southern Virginia, although some have charged it to his ambition to achieve independent command. While he was away from the Army of Northern Virginia, Hooker moved against Lee and the Battle of Chancellorsville, May 1–4, resulted. With this evidence of the opening of active campaigning Lee recalled Longstreet. It was then that Haskell was ordered to Longstreet.

18.   While Longstreet was making the effort to collect supplies in North Carolina he maintained his headquarters at Suffolk, which is in southeast Virginia near the North Carolina border.

19.   Matthias Winston Henry graduated from West Point with the class of 1861 and took part in the training of recruits for the Federal army at Carlisle Barracks and Washington until his resignation, August 3, when he gave the excuse of ill-health. Although he appears frequently in the *Official Records* after his first listing as a lieutenant with Pelham's Battery in an action on August 28, 1862, little information about him seems available.

20.   John Pelham of Alabama is one of the romantic figures of the Confederacy. He resigned as a last-year man at West Point, April 22, 1861, and entered the Confederate service about a month later. His personality appealed to all with whom he came in contact —brave and modest, youthful and handsome, he drew but one criticism: some called him a flirt! He served with distinction as commander of Stuart's Horse Artillery, and at Fredericksburg not only won Lee's high praise but the name which still sticks to him, "the gallant Pelham." He died in action at Kelly's Ford, Virginia, March 17, 1863, and in death received promotion to lieutenant colonel, a tribute to his devotion, courage, and skill.

21.   Haskell's statement is confirmed by the report of Gettysburg by Major B. F. Eshleman of the Washington (Louisiana) Artillery.

22. Brandy Station was a few miles north of Culpeper Court House on the Orange and Alexandria Railroad, while Stevensburg was off the railroad somewhat farther to the east. Brandy Station, also referred to occasionally as Fleetwood Heights, was fought June 9, 1863, between the Federal cavalry under Pleasanton and the Confederates of Stuart, who had been gathered the day before for a grand review.

23. Matthew C. Butler was one of seven brothers in the Confederate army. At the time of Brandy Station he commanded the Second South Carolina Cavalry. He served with the Army of Northern Virginia until he joined the campaign against Sherman in the Carolinas in 1865. He became a major general in September 1864, a rank he also held in the United States Army in the Spanish-American War of 1898.

24. A brother of Wade Hampton, Frank Hampton was lieutenant colonel of the 2nd South Carolina Cavalry when killed.

25. James J. Iredell, 53rd North Carolina Infantry.

26. Charles W. McCreary, major, later colonel, 1st South Carolina Infantry, was not killed at Gettysburg.

27. The Federal general, Gouverneur K. Warren, then Chief Engineer of the Army of the Potomac, at the direction of General Meade made a visit to Little Round Top, apparently but a short time after Haskell was there. He moved troops to occupy it in time to resist the Confederate effort to seize it.

28. Daniel E. Sickles of New York had won notoriety before the war when he shot and killed Philip Barton Key, son of the composer and author of "The Star-Spangled Banner," because of Key's attentions to Mrs. Sickles. Sickles secured a commission in the army for political reasons, and though he was without military experience rose from colonel to major general. At Gettysburg he was in command of a corps and received a serious wound, losing a leg as a consequence. He was accused of poor generalship in the battle and was removed from active service.

29. Chickamauga, fought September 18–20, 1863, was one of the few times the Confederates attempted to use their interior lines for battle purposes. Longstreet's corps left Virginia to join with Bragg's army in Tennessee and some troops from Johnston in Mississippi to fight the Federal Army of the Cumberland in North Georgia.

The result was a victory on the field, although Bragg's failure to follow it up allowed the Federals to recover and two months later in the series of battles about Chattanooga to drive the Confederates into Georgia.

30. Evander McIver Law, a South Carolinian, was a schoolteacher who entered Confederate service as a captain. His father and both his grandfathers had served with Francis Marion, the "Swamp Fox," in the Revolution. He made an excellent record in every command assignment, and became a brigadier general at 26. At Gettysburg he was among those who sought the occupation of Little Round Top before the Federals took it, and he later wrote that the Confederates lost the battle because of the failure to occupy it and its accompanying height, Round Top. At the close of the war, he was with Johnston, opposing Sherman in North Carolina.

31. Edward P. Alexander of Georgia, West Point '57, by his physical appearance gave more the impression of a scholar than a man of action, yet as an artillerist he grew steadily in the appreciation of his associates and his commanders. Alexander, an engineer officer at the time, collaborated with A. J. Meyer, a surgeon, in 1859 to devise the American wigwag system, which remained an important part of military field communication until the introduction of the walkie-talkie in World War II. His *Military Memoirs of a Confederate*, which is a critical evaluation of Confederate operations as well as a narrative of Alexander's own experiences, is among the most valuable discussions of the war.

32. Longstreet, in his own account, states that he felt so keenly what the result would be that he could not give Pickett a verbal order, but indicated it "by an affirmative bow," when Pickett asked if he should start the attack.

33. Henry Jackson Hunt, West Point '39, as a member of an army board had devised new light artillery tactics before the war. From his first experience in engagement at Manassas, Hunt displayed the ability which made him pre-eminent as an artillery commander. Prompt and decisive in action, he showed an efficiency in the provision of ammunition for his guns and intelligence in their tactical arrangements. Perhaps his finest hour was at Gettysburg, where he broke the back of Pickett's attack and gave the victory to the Union forces.

34. Haskell's description of his part in the artillery support of Pickett's charge is borne out by the report of Major Eshleman of the Washington (Louisiana) Artillery (see *O. R.,* Series I, v. XXVII, pt. 2, pp. 433-436) and Alexander in his *Military Memoirs,* pp. 425, 428-429.

35. There is much dispute and has been about where Pickett was in the charge which bears his name. Haskell reports where he saw Pickett and his staff. The barn was apparently that of the Codori family.

36. George Gordon Meade, West Point '35, like many other army engineers, had served the nation by assisting in the building of railroads and improving navigable streams and harbor facilities before the war. Never tactful, he consistently had difficulties with other officers, but recognition of his ability and his steadfast character was of constant help. He was not Lincoln's first choice for the command of the Army of the Potomac in June 1863, but the refusal of General John F. Reynolds to accept the assignment brought it to Meade. From his letters to his wife it would appear that Meade made an unquestioned effort to impress both President and Mrs. Lincoln but when the news came of his elevation—in the middle of the night as the armies moved to their climactic meeting at Gettysburg—Meade protested his incapacity. But he typically proceeded to do his best in the task given him.

37. Henry Heth of Virginia, West Point '47, was attractive personally, but his reputation as a commander outran his achievements. It was Heth's desire to secure the shoes which he heard were ready for the taking in Gettysburg that brought the two armies together and gave fame to the quiet little Pennsylvania community.

38. Pettigrew died July 17, 1863, from a wound received the night of July 13-14.

39. William Dorsey Pender of North Carolina, West Point '54, as a colonel of infantry at Seven Pines won the admiration of President Davis who addressed him on the field, *"General* Pender, I salute you." Only 29 when he became a major general in May 1863, Pender died of wounds received at Gettysburg, his first battle after his promotion. Lee said of him: "His promise and usefulness as an officer were only equalled by the purity and excellence of his private life."

40. In his report of Gettysburg, Colonel Abner Perrin, then commanding McGowan's Brigade, said of William Haskell: "He was educated and accomplished, possessing in a high degree every virtuous quality of the true gentleman and Christian. He was an officer of the most excellent judgment, and a soldier of the coolest and most chivalrous daring."

41. At the start of the war in 1861 many Southerners had the strange misconception that the war would be something of an outing and of short duration. With no military experience, some overstocked themselves with personal belongings, which under the exigencies of campaigning they abandoned with no more thought of the future than they had shown when reporting. Others came with nothing more than the clothes they wore, relying on a government which was inadequately prepared to take care of them. Lack of manufacturing facilities and the Federal blockade made it difficult if not impossible to overcome deficiencies, the most pressing of which consistently was insufficient medical supplies.

Possibly the greatest handicap to the Confederate service of supply other than the two mentioned, was Lucius B. Northrop, whom Davis chose to head it. Northrop, West Point '31 and a native of South Carolina, had turned to the practice of medicine in the 1840's, and had no training of any consequence for the position he occupied in the Confederate army. A vain, obstinate, argumentative individual, he was in constant difficulties with the commanders in the field. He started by insisting in 1861–1862 that all food, even when gathered in the area occupied by the army in Virginia, should be sent to Richmond and then reshipped to the army. Later, outside Virginia, he forced the army commanders to supply their men from the areas in which they were, but he sent agents from Richmond to compete for the purchase of the available food. State rivalry, the loss of productive territory, depreciated currency, and deteriorating transportation intensified Northrop's inefficient conduct of his office, which caused men as early as the fall of 1863 to talk of the failure of the Confederacy.

42. The election of Nathaniel P. Banks as speaker of the House in 1856 was hailed as the first major defeat of the political supporters of slavery in a quarter of a century. In that position he conducted himself ably and efficiently. He received a commission as a major general of volunteers on the outbreak of the war, but like most of the political appointees he found military campaigns more difficult than those for office. Jackson easily outwitted and defeated him in the Shenandoah Valley in 1862.

43. Philip H. Sheridan, West Point '43, like many men of small stature, was an aggressive, ambitious individual. He had an interesting career in the war, starting as a quartermaster in the secondary area of Missouri and ending as commander of the cavalry corps of the Army of the Potomac. It was his attack which at Five Forks in April 1865 broke the back of the Confederate defense of Petersburg. He then kept such pressure on the Confederates that they could not form a defense line. Sheridan's rise was surprisingly quick. He became a colonel in May 1862 and by December of that year was a major general.

44. The Federal policy to which Haskell refers was laid down by Halleck in letters to commanders in Tennessee and Mississippi in March 1863. "We must live upon the enemy's country as much as possible, and destroy his supplies," wrote the then Federal general in chief. "This is cruel warfare, but the enemy has brought it on himself." See O. R., v. XXIV, pt. 3, pp. 157, 309.

45. Criticism of "West Pointism," as it was called, was frequent in the Confederacy but it was usually laid at Davis's door, not Lee's. Lee had only the power to recommend, and Davis usually followed his own wishes in elevating men. The truth is that, while not all the West Pointers proved to be capable commanders, the South would have been under a severe handicap without Johnston, Lee, Jackson, Stuart, and any number of other Academy graduates.

46. Promotions, by act of the Congress, March 1861, had to be by the President, acting with the advice of Congress, and except for the elections held when the regiments were reorganized in early 1862, were to follow seniority. By an act passed in January 1862, the President could promote for acts of unusual gallantry. But there was no way for an officer to be promoted on the field by a superior.

47. At the start of the war, John B. Gordon, a young man of 29, operated a coal mine in the mountains of the northwest corner of Georgia. There among his neighbors he raised a company, to which they gave the name Raccoon Roughs, for the nearby Raccoon Mountain. Under the command of Gordon it went to Virginia before First Manassas, and Gordon, whose wife accompanied him throughout the war, served with the Army of Northern Virginia until the surrender at Appomattox. In spite of his lack of

training, his intelligence and military aptitude won promotion for him, and at the end of the war he was a major general, and commanded a wing of Lee's army. Courtly in manner, tall and impressive, he was a courageous, aggressive fighter. As one of his men said of him: "He's most the prettiest thing you ever did see on a field of fight. It 'ud put fight into a whipped chicken just to look at him."

48.   The Wilderness, the opening phase of Grant's 1864 campaign, was fought May 5, 6, 7.

49.   Gordon's promotion had the dual purpose of recognizing his valuable work of May 6 and his merits as a leader, which Lee thought superior to others, whom he transferred so there would be no conflict of seniority.

50.   An ambitious, gallant South Carolinian, Perrin won the admiration of his men for his bravery. He succeeded to the command of the brigade known successively as Gregg's and MacGowan's at Chancellorsville, when MacGowan received serious wounds. He died in action at Spotsylvania, May 12, 1864.

51.   There were two groups, the Bucktails and the Bogus Bucktails, among the Pennsylvanians. The first was the 42nd Infantry, which joined up at the start of the war, and resented it when later the 149th and 150th regiments took the name. The men of the 42nd dubbed the others "Bogus" Bucktails, but so gallant was the work of the newer Bucktails at Gettysburg that "Bogus" was dropped.

52.   Perrin's promotion came September 17, 1863, to rank from September 10, not from the date of Gettysburg. It was confirmed by the Senate February 17, 1864.

53.   The differences between Lee and Longstreet over battle tactics at Gettysburg on both the second and third days are tragic examples of Lee's failure to force the compliance of his obstinate subordinate. On the second day Longstreet's recommendation was to move around the left flank of the Federals. On the third, he opposed Pickett's charge, which he could not see as succeeding.

54.   The Confederate Congress authorized the President, in an act approved October 13, 1862, "to bestow medals, with proper devices, upon such officers of the armies of the Confederate States as shall be conspicuous for courage and good conduct on the field of battle, and also to confer a badge of distinction upon one private or non-commissioned officer of each company after every signal

victory it shall have assisted to achieve." In practice, the award of medals and badges became a listing on a roll of honor, which was sometimes delayed as much as two years. For example, those who received the distinction for participation in Sharpsburg were on lists published August 10, 1864, and December 10, 1864, by which time practically every man had died or been killed. No reason is given for the failure to award medals except that difficulties in procuring them prevented it. Sometimes the companies refused to designate one of their company for the distinction, apparently believing that all had been equally gallant, or that a number had been. For some reason the fact that a way to honor gallant conduct and bravery had been provided failed to make an impression generally, and one frequently finds a statement similar to that of Haskell, that anything comparable to the Medal of Honor was not provided in the Confederate army.

Chapter 5.

1. The movement of Longstreet's corps from Virginia to North Georgia to join Bragg's Army of Tennessee in the Battle of Chickamauga against Rosecrans' Army of the Cumberland, September 19–20, 1863, was the most important use of its railroads and interior lines by the Confederacy in the war. The troops began to arrive September 18 after a long trip, which started September 9, but Longstreet himself did not reach the battlefield until midnight, September 19–20. He took command of the Confederate left wing, and his attack, which started around noon on the 20th, broke the Federal line and gave the Southerners the victory, the only conclusive victory of major proportions to be won in the West by the Confederates.

Bragg, however, failed to take advantage of the enemy's defeat. Longstreet and others of the subordinate generals did their best to persuade Bragg to move against the disorganized Federals, huddled in Chattanooga, but without success. As a consequence, they petitioned Davis for a new commanding general for the Army of Tennessee. This aroused the antagonism of Bragg, who at the first opportunity—and against the instructions of Davis—sent Longstreet with his troops to operate against Knoxville. Bragg then lost Chattanooga to the Federals under Grant, Thomas and Sherman, and retreated into Georgia. Longstreet remained in East Tennessee for the winter and rejoined the Army of Northern Virginia in April

1864, in time to take part in the campaign which Grant initiated the next month.

2. Bristoe Station occurred October 14, 1863.

3. John R. Cooke was not a graduate of West Point, although he had been a commissioned officer in the United States Army. He was a son of Philip St. George Cooke and the brother-in-law of Jeb Stuart. The elder Cooke, although a Virginian, remained in the Federal army, but saw no active service after the Peninsula campaign of 1862.

4. William W. Kirkland of North Carolina was so severely wounded as a regimental commander in the Valley campaign of 1862 that he did not return to duty until Gettysburg. His wound at Bristoe Station was so severe that he was again incapacitated for a year. His service after his return to duty in 1864 was first with Longstreet on the north side of the James River in the Petersburg defense, but in December 1864 he was transferred to North Carolina where he remained until the surrender in April 1865.

5. The Confederate mishap at Bristoe Station was a consequence of A. P. Hill's eagerness to attack before he made a sufficient reconnaissance. The retreating V Corps of the Federal army held the attention of Hill, who was surprised to find the II Corps in position to hit the two Confederate brigades. Hill took the whole blame for the failure in his report to Lee, who upon examining the field next day displayed his feeling by saying at last, "Well, well, General, bury these poor men and let us say no more about it."

6. Lee hoped that Meade intended an attack when the Federals moved in November 1863 toward the Confederates and prepared an extensive system of earthworks along the little stream called Mine Run, about 12 miles north of Orange Court House, to receive the enemy assault. But the Northerners, after some rather heavy skirmishing, on viewing the strength of the Southern position, gave up the campaign, just as Lee himself determined to assume the offensive. When the Confederates moved forward on December 2, they found that the Federals had recrossed the Rapidan River.

7. Green Spring Valley is east of Charlottesville and south of Gordonsville.

8. The Wilderness, true to its name, was a tangle of underbrush and forest, approximately 15 miles square, south of the Rapidan River and west of Fredericksburg. Grant's campaign, which opened here

on May 5, was planned to coincide with that of Sherman in Georgia against the Army of Tennessee under Johnston. From that time on, unrelenting pressure was kept on the two main armies of the Confederacy by the Federals.

9. Joseph Hooker, West Point '37, won the nickname of Fighting Joe in the Peninsula Campaign. He was an affable, physically attractive individual, who received the command of the Army of the Potomac after Burnside's failure at Fredericksburg. But at the same time Lincoln rebuked him because of reports that Hooker had been unduly critical of his superiors. Unfortunately for Hooker, he proved no more of a match for Lee than any of the earlier commanders of the Army of the Potomac, and at Chancellorsville was soundly whipped. He was then sent to Tennessee, where he aided in the relief of Chattanooga, but before Atlanta became disgruntled over Howard's elevation over him and resigned from the service.

10. James S. Wadsworth, a wealthy politician of upper New York State, was of middle age when the war began. He commanded a division in the Battle of Gettysburg and held the Confederates on the first day despite heavy losses among his men. In the Battle of the Wilderness he had two horses shot under him before he was himself fatally wounded. He died two days later in a Confederate field hospital.

11. In memory, Haskell condensed the rapidly occurring events in this tense action. Dr. Freeman in *Lee's Lieutenants*, Vol. III, p. 361, calls Longstreet's conference with Lee "brief," which under the pressing circumstances it must have been. Because of the confusion of Haskell's memory of events, Freeman ignores the statement that Jenkins and Mahone were present.

12. Micah Jenkins, a South Carolina schoolteacher, was considered by Longstreet one of the finest officers in the army: "His taste and talents were for military service. He was intelligent, quick, untiring, attentive, zealous in the discharge of duty, truly faithful to official obligations, abreast with the foremost in battle, and withal a humble, noble Christian." He received his death wounds at the Wilderness almost as he finished telling Longstreet that he had been despondent about the war's outcome but had lost his feeling of worry in the triumph of the day.

13. William Mahone of Virginia, a small, ambitious man, had initiated a large enterprise—the creation of a single system of the small

railroads between Norfolk and Bristol, Tennessee—when the war intervened to prevent its accomplishment. His career as a brigadier was generally undistinguished, but he earned distinction in command of a division. His gallant work in repulsing the enemy after the explosion at the Crater before Petersburg won the recommendation of Lee for promotion to major general. After the war he re-entered railroading but was diverted into politics.

14. Osmun Latrobe of Maryland was a member of Longstreet's staff from the Peninsula campaign on. His fellow staff member, Sorrel, says that Latrobe was "as big in body and frame as he was in heart." Latrobe succeeded Sorrel as Longstreet's chief of staff, when Sorrel was promoted to brigadier general and assigned elsewhere in October 1864.

15. Haskell, in his brief account of the Wilderness, wrote from memory and his own knowledge of events. As both were limited to the sector of the field and the incidents which came under his observation, he omits some matters of importance. He says nothing, for example, of the remarkable participation in the battle of Sorrel, who led the flank attack against the Federal left and won high praise and promotion later to a brigadier general as a consequence. It was Sorrel, too, who seems to have first reached Lee with Longstreet's message, although Latrobe, despite the wounds he received earlier, doubtless took part in the search for the army commander. While Haskell was away, looking for Lee, Longstreet turned the command of the corps over to Major General Charles W. Field, one of his division commanders who was close at hand when Longstreet received his wounds. R. H. Anderson, who was the senior division commander, was put in charge of the corps on the next day, May 7.

16. These two events, one on May 2, 1863, and the other May 6, 1864, occurred in the same general area. It is interesting to conjecture what might have happened to Grant, had this opening battle of his 1864 campaign in Virginia turned into a repulse similar to that of Hooker at Chancellorsville a year before. Without the accidental wounding of Longstreet and Jenkins, it might easily have happened.

17. Spotsylvania, the second of the great battles in Virginia that May, lasted from the 8th to the 18th. At the start, the Federals thought they had passed the Confederates' right to get between them and

Richmond, but the cavalry, aided by Haskell's artillery battalion, intervened until the infantry were in position.

18. Alexander, in *Military Memoirs,* p. 510, describes the Block House as being a "peculiar looking house, . . . built of squared logs."

19. John R. Potts of North Carolina.

20. On May 9 Sheridan started a cavalry raid which took him almost to Richmond. Stuart divided his troops, placing one group in the rear of Sheridan, to harass the Federals, while the other, under Stuart himself, raced to get ahead of the advancing enemy. Stuart beat Sheridan to Yellow Tavern, and in the engagement which followed the Federals' arrival, Stuart was mortally wounded and died the next day, May 13, in Richmond.

21. Haskell here refers to May 12, although there was another attack by Grant at the Bloody Angle on May 19.

22. Major David Watson, who was at his death second in command of Hardaway's Artillery Battalion of A. P. Hill's corps, was given high praise for his work at the Bloody Angle.

23. Daniel was mortally wounded, not killed, at the Bloody Angle, although his appearance in the hasty glance Haskell had may have left that impression. Daniel died the next day, May 13.

24. Cold Harbor opened June 1 in a fight which brought light casualties as compared with those of June 3, the day of the tragic assault which Grant always regretted having ordered. The area was so dominated by Confederate fire that it was impossible to make the single, heavy attack Grant intended. The result was a series of semi-isolated movements as troops found it possible to get up and attempt to advance. This gave the impression of repeated attacks, such as Haskell describes. The Confederate fire was so heavy and sustained that men could neither advance nor retreat, but were pinned wherever they could find cover. The report was widespread afterwards that the men finally refused to accept orders to move forward, as Haskell indicates, but Alexander, *Military Memoirs,* p. 541, denies this. Union losses at Cold Harbor totaled around 13,000, while those of the Confederates are estimated at hardly a third that number.

25. Actually the Confederate position extended from White Oak Swamp to Malvern Hill, where Lee's army still covered the way

to Richmond and was able quickly to cross the James, should Grant go that way.

26. Bermuda Hundred, on the south side of the James River, is but a few miles from Petersburg. The action here was June 14–15.

27. On June 16, Beauregard moved into the lines at Petersburg, which Lee reached June 18. Field's division, of which Haskell's battalion was a part, was at Petersburg early that morning.

Chapter 6.

1. The possibility of running an underground shaft from the Federal lines to lay a mine under the Confederate works attracted men of the 48th Pennsylvania, which had a number of coal miners in its ranks. They suggested the idea to their commander, who sent it along to the higher echelons. Military men were somewhat incredulous that such an effort could be successful. But permission was granted, and the men started work June 25. A month later the shaft was complete and the mine laid. The main shaft was 510 feet long, with laterals of around 35 feet to the right and left at its end. Although the builders wanted to use a charge of 14,000 pounds of powder in the mine, only 8,000 were allotted. The mine was set off early on the morning of July 30, and the air was filled, according to the accounts, with men, guns, artillery carriages, and a conglomerate debris, all of which showered on attackers and defenders alike. The Union troops were so startled by the immensity of the explosion that they delayed their assault for a while. Why the combination of surprise and devastating force should not have been successful is attributable, in General Alexander's opinion, to the large number of Federals who were gathered to rush forward. There were so many, he said, that they got in each other's way. The outcome was practically a total failure for the Federals, whose losses were about 4 times those of the Confederates. The Crater measured roughly about 30 feet deep, with lateral dimensions of about 60 feet by 150.

2. Stephen Elliott, Jr., a native of South Carolina, was the son of the first Episcopal Bishop of Georgia. Until mid-1864, his service was in the Charleston area. His wounds, which he received on July 30, incapacitated him for further service and eventually caused his death in March 1866 at his home in Beaufort, South Carolina.

3. Elliott commanded at Fort Sumter from September 1863 until sent to Virginia in May 1864.

4. Major Wade H. Gibbes, West Point '60, is given credit by Schaff for having fired the first gun on Sumter, something which is usually attributed to Edmund Ruffin. The wounds he received at the Crater kept Gibbes out of action until the following February, after which he commanded the artillery at Chaffin's Bluff.

5. Lieutenant Colonel Frank Huger, West Point '60, was the son of Major General Benjamin Huger, who was the victim of Longstreet's failure to follow orders at Seven Pines. Frank Huger served as an artillery officer with the Army of Northern Virginia through the war, except for the time he was with Longstreet in Tennessee, and received commendation for his conduct in several important engagements.

6. James N. Lamkin served as commander of the Nelson (Virginia) Light Artillery in South Carolina and with the Army of Northern Virginia. He was assigned to Haskell's Battalion in command of a battery bearing his name in 1864, and was one of those recommended by Alexander for promotion to major in March 1865.

7. A small type of mortar.

8. The artillery arm received full credit for having prevented a major catastrophe at the Crater and high in the list of officers commended was John Haskell. Divisional commander, General B. R. Johnson, praised him for his "prompt and efficient co-operation" and General Pendleton, chief of artillery of the Army of Northern Virginia, noted in his report: "Major Haskell, with conspicuous gallantry, taking personal charge of 12-pounders, moved them forward to the trenches within 50 yards of the crater, so as to render their fire particularly accurate and destructive."

9. Fort Harrison, which was about a mile from Chaffin's Bluff on the James in the Confederate defense line, was taken by the Federals September 29, 1864. This endangered the James River approach to Richmond, and on the next day the Confederates made a desperate effort to retake it, but failed. On October 1 additional Southern troops, including Haskell's Battalion of artillery, crossed the river from the Petersburg side, to make another attempt to recapture this important part of the Richmond defenses. This effort, known as the Battle of Darbytown Road, was on October 7 and also failed. In it John Haskell barely escaped serious injury,

but received only a grazing wound on the head from a minie ball, but his brother, Aleck, was very seriously wounded, losing an eye by a wound which the doctors thought would inevitably be fatal. Haskell says that he had written earlier about this engagement, but it must have been lost before transcription, as the account is in none of the manuscripts.

10. W. R. Johnson was a prominent resident of Petersburg, who was known as the "Napoleon of the turf."

11. Burgess's Mill was about eight miles southwest of Petersburg, where the Boydston Plank Road crossed Hatcher's Run. The action there occurred October 27.

12. William Preston Hampton, who had enlisted as a private in Hampton's Legion at 17 on the outbreak of the war, became a lieutenant on his father's staff after the Seven Days. When General Hampton heard of his being wounded at Burgess's Mill he rushed to Preston's side. He quickly realized the hopelessness of the wound, "kissed his brave boy, wiped a tear from his eye," and resumed his pressing task of directing the action against the enemy. A group gathered around the dying Preston and quickly attracted the attention of Union soldiers, who concentrated fire on them, severely wounding Wade Hampton, Jr. Somewhat later, a report came to headquarters that an officer was lying, severely wounded, nearby, but scouts failed to find him. After a time Barker dragged himself into the open, and the division's chief surgeon declared him too badly wounded to live. Fortunately, the result was different, and Barker recovered. He had served on Hampton's staff until the South Carolinian succeeded to Stuart's command of the cavalry of the Army of Northern Virginia. After that, Barker served on the staff of General Mathew C. Butler, who took Hampton's place as a division commander.

13. Winfield Scott Hancock, West Point '44, was conspicuous in every quality as a commander. Thorough in details, intelligent in organization and preparation of plans, he also was a dynamic leader. In his account of Gettysburg, Frank Haskell said that Hancock was the "tallest and most shapely" of the Federal generals. "I think that if he were in citizens' clothes, and should give commands in the army to those who did not know him, he would be likely to be obeyed at once." Although he never exercised independent command, the consensus of opinion among his contemporaries was that he would have done well, whatever the assignment.

14. Reams' Station, about 12 miles south of Petersburg on the Petersburg and Weldon railroad, was the scene of heavy fighting on August 24. Although generally accounted a Southern victory, the fighting failed to re-establish Confederate control of the railroad.

15. Hill had been away from his command for ten days because of another of his recurrent attacks of illness, when he returned just in time to take part in the effort to re-form the lines after Sheridan's attack at Five Forks on April 1. Early the next morning Hill rode to General Lee's Headquarters, accompanied only by some couriers, and then toward the Confederate right. With only his sergeant of couriers, G. W. Tucker, Hill came on a small group of Federal soldiers, well within the Southern lines. Without hesitation he rode toward them, to demand their surrender. They fired and Hill fell, killed by a shot just over the heart.

16. Pegram won the name "the boy artillerist" by his youth, According to Gordon McCabe, his poor eyesight was responsible for his close fighting, as he insisted on being able to see the enemy. He stated that he would never lose a gun unless his body lay before it, a statement borne out by the event, for he lost both his first gun and his life at Five Forks.

17. Thomas L. Rosser, Virginia-born but living in Texas when appointed to West Point, resigned upon his graduation in '61. He won attention in the Peninsula campaign as an artillerist by shooting down a Federal observation balloon. After being wounded in the Seven Days at Mechanicsville he entered the cavalry, and was promoted to the command of Ashby's brigade after Gettysburg. He was with Early in the Shenandoah Valley as a major general, but joined the army at Petersburg in early '65. Before the surrender he with his troops cut their way through the Federals, but surrendered a few days later near Hanover Court House. Pelham, as has already been noted, resigned before graduating from West Point.

18. Pierce M. B. Young was a student at West Point but resigned when Georgia, his home state, seceded. Starting as a lieutenant of artillery, he ended the war as a major general of cavalry. Courtly in his personal relationships, he was a fearless leader in action, and when separated once from his troops, he rode straight through the intervening Federals, cutting an enemy officer across the face with a switch. Young was sent to Georgia in 1864 to defend Augusta against attack by Sherman. At the end of the war, he was in the Carolinas, campaigning against the advancing Federals.

19. George A. Custer, most celebrated for his defeat by the Western Indians at Little Big Horn, where he and his command were wiped out in 1876, graduated from West Point just as the war began. His first battle experience was at First Manassas, where he arrived the morning of the engagement. He was tall and slender, and his long blond hair and mustache made him conspicuous in appearance, something he accentuated by a colorful uniform, which included a cavalier hat and a large scarlet tie.

20. Of Pelham's officers mentioned by Haskell, Lieutenant Colonel R. Preston Chew commanded the artillery of Fitzhugh Lee's Cavalry Corps at the end of the war, while Major James Breathed commanded a battalion. Captain M. W. Henry, as has been noted, left the Army of Northern Virginia for the Trans-Mississippi Department after Gettysburg. Major James W. Thomson, also an artilleryman with Lee's Corps, was killed at Rice's Station April 6, 1865, while leading a cavalry charge. Major William M. McGregor was with the army at Petersburg, but his battery is listed at Appomattox without a commander.

Chapter 7.

1. Lee's order to Ewell of April 2, 1865, directed him to move south of the James River that night by bridges at or near Richmond.

2. These guns were named for their inventor, Sir William George Armstrong, and were rifled breechloaders.

3. Samuel Preston Moore had served for 26 years in the medical department of the United States Army when he resigned in 1861, and began practice in Little Rock. He accepted the position as Surgeon General of the Confederate forces in July 1861, and for the four years of the war worked steadfastly to overcome the grave handicaps of the Southern medical services. He instituted examinations, by which he got rid of incompetents and discovered the more capable for key positions. He organized the Association of Army and Navy Surgeons of the Confederate States, and by its meetings spread more quickly new methods and techniques. He was largely responsible for the creation and publication of the *Confederate States Surgical and Medical Journal,* which he attempted to distribute as widely as possible. He instigated the writing and publishing of *A Manual of Military Surgery* and *Re-*

*sources of the Southern Fields and Forests, Medical, Economical,
and Agricultural.* By the second of these he hoped to fill in some
degree the shortage of medicines which the blockade caused. He
modified hospital arrangements, and in other ways proved so
industrious and capable an administrator that one wonders why he
has not received more attention in the writings about the war.

4. Langdon; Alexander; Charles; William; John; Joseph; Lewis.

5. Robert F. Mason.

6. Cameron was a prominent tobacco manufacturer, who built a
   pretentious home, Mt. Erin, at Petersburg in the war.

7. Although there was no official designation of Alexander as the
   army's chief of artillery, his report of a conversation he had with
   Lee the morning of April 8 indicates that he was acting in that
   capacity.

8. Henry L. Benning, who had graduated from the University of
   Georgia with the highest honors in his class of 1834, was a supreme
   court justice of Georgia from 1853 to 1859, and worked earnestly
   for the secession of his state in the convention of January 1861.
   Although without military experience, his coolness, steadfastness,
   and daring won admiration from his men. He was with the First
   Corps in all its campaigns, except for the time necessary to recover
   from severe wounds received at the Wilderness. At Chickamauga,
   in a disastrous moment in the fighting, he reported to Longstreet
   that everything was ruined for him, that he didn't have a man left.
   Longstreet looked closely at him, then said that surely Benning
   could find one man somewhere. When he did, he should report
   back, and Longstreet would assign him a place for his "brigade"
   in the line. The answer brought back Benning's confidence, and he
   soon was again in the thick of the fight.

9. Martin W. Gary, a graduate of Harvard, was an earnest advocate
   of secession in South Carolina and went into the military forces
   immediately the state seceded. He was with Hampton's Legion,
   rising through grades from captain to colonel. A brigadier general
   of cavalry after June 1864, his troops were the last to leave Richmond, with the enemy already in sight. Gary made his way to
   Greenboro, N.C., after refusing to stay at Appomattox for the surrender, and formed an escort for Davis and the Cabinet, whom he
   accompanied until they reached his home at Cokesbury. S.C.

10. Lee had made no "demands" on Grant, but the passage of communications between the two on April 7 and 8 probably led to that interpretation.

11. Major General Andrew A. Humphreys, West Point '31, was a Pennsylvanian who became prominently known for his engineering work in hydraulics and flood control before the war. He proved a capable field commander with the Union army, but after 1865 returned to engineering and science, in which he won a national and international reputation.

12. Charles C. Marshall was a member of the same family as Chief Justice Marshall. He was practicing law in Baltimore at the outbreak of the war, but immediately sought a place with the Confederate army. Ill health intervened, however, to keep him inactive until March 1862, when he became a member of Lee's staff. Lee assigned him the task of preparing reports and other documents, and worked so closely with him that no other probably knew so well the attitudes and opinions of the general.

13. In this report of his carrying Longstreet's message to Lee, Haskell —who was writing entirely from memory—seems wrong in such details as reporting that Fitz Lee had broken through an enemy line. Apparently Lee said that he had found a point where he thought it could be broken. Generally Haskell's account agrees with the others.

14. Longstreet says in his account of this incident that Custer came to him with Captain Sims, and it is probably that both accounts are correct: that Sims met Custer first, as Longstreet describes, and that Custer then saw Gibbes, who had been a class ahead of Custer at West Point.

Chapter 8.

1. As Grant moved frequently in this crucial period, the spot where Lee was waiting when Haskell delivered the message from Longstreet proved out of the way. Because of this Lee changed his place of waiting, so it is possible that this conversation with Haskell took place in this interim. But if it were after the meeting with Grant, Haskell is wrong about the elapsed time. Grant reached the McLean house about 1:30 P.M. and Lee left around 4.

2. Lee's order to Haskell did not mean to arrange the official details of the surrender, as the three Confederate commissioners for that purpose were Gordon, Longstreet, and Pendleton, but to assist in their preparation and to carry them out.

3. Major Wilmer McLean, who lived on the field of Manassas in 1861, after that battle moved to Appomattox, where he felt he would be safe from military operations. On April 9 he encountered Colonel Marshall, whom Lee had sent to secure a place for the meeting with Grant. McLean at first suggested an unoccupied house in bad condition and appearance, but upon Marshall's objection offered his own. As a result souvenir hunters raided the nicely furnished home, proving almost as ruinous as battle had at Manassas.

4. Bvt. Major General Charles Griffin, West Point '47, began the war as commander of a battery which he raised among the enlisted garrison at West Point, where he was an instructor. In their first engagement at First Manassas, the command was nearly wiped out, when a group of Confederates were mistakenly identified as Federals and were allowed to approach without opposition. Griffin was arrogant and controversial, but his ability won him steady advancement. He commanded the 5th Corps at Appomattox.

5. Bvt. Major General Joseph J. Bartlett commanded the 1st Division, Vth Corps, at Appomattox. He was not a professional soldier, but volunteered for service with New York troops on the outbreak of the war, and served effectively in all grades from company commander to division commander. Like Haskell, Bartlett was not a member of the official Commission which consisted of three men for each army. To meet with Gordon, Longstreet and Pendleton, Grant appointed Gibbon, Griffin and Bvt. Major General Wesley Merritt. Merritt, a graduate of West Point in 1860, was a cavalry officer, the commander of the cavalry of the Army of the Shenandoah.

6. Although the youngest member of Lee's staff, Taylor, a Virginian, who joined Lee in May 1861, was the only officer to serve steadily on it until the close of the war. On the day that the Confederates gave up Petersburg and Richmond, Taylor—with Lee's permission —rode to the capital to meet his sweetheart. He married her that night, and leaving her to the care of friends hastened to rejoin the army on the retreat.

Selective Bibliography

Alexander, E. P., *Military Memoirs of a Confederate*. New York: Charles Scribner's Sons, 1907.

Bennett, Susan Smythe, comp., "The Cheves Family of South Carolina," *South Carolina Historical and Genealogical Magazine*, vol. XXXV, #3, p. 79-95.

Brooks, Ulysses R., *Butler and His Cavalry in the War of Secession, 1861–1865*. Columbia: State Company, 1909.

Caldwell, J. F. J., *The History of a Brigade of South Carolinians, Known First as "Gregg's," and Subsequently as "McGowan's Brigade."* Philadelphia: King and Baird, 1866.

Chamberlayne, John H., *Ham Chamberlayne—Virginian*. Richmond: Dietz Printing Company, 1932.

Chesnut, M. B., *A Diary from Dixie*, edited by Ben Ames Williams. Boston: Houghton, Mifflin Company, 1949.

Cooper, Walter G., *The Story of Georgia*. New York: American Historical Society, 1938.

Crawford, Samuel W., *The Genesis of the Civil War*. New York: C. L. Webster and Co., 1887.

Cunningham, H. H., *Doctors in Gray*. Baton Rouge: Louisiana State University Press, 1958.

Dale, Louise Haskell, *Alexander Cheves Haskell: The Portrait of a Man*. Privately printed, 1934.

DeLeon, T. C., *Belles, Beaux, and Brains of the 60's*. New York: G. W. Dillingham Company, 1907.

Dictionary of American Biography, edited by Dumas Malone. New York: Charles Scribner's Sons, 1928–1936.

Eliot, Ellesworth, Jr., *West Point in the Confederacy*. New York: G. A. Baker and Co., 1941.

Estes, Claud, comp., *List of Field Officers, Regiments and Battalions in the Confederate States Army, 1861–1865*. Macon, Georgia: J. W. Burke Co., 1912.

Evans, Clement A., ed., *Confederate Military History*. Atlanta: Confederate Publishing Company, 1899.

Freeman, Douglas Southall, *R. E. Lee*. New York: Charles Scribner's Sons, 1934–1935.

Freeman, Douglas Southall, *Lee's Lieutenants*. New York: Charles Scribner's Sons, 1942–1944.

Gordon, John B., *Reminiscences of the Civil War*. New York: Charles Scribner's Sons, 1903.

Hagood, Johnson, *Memoirs of the War of Secession*. Columbia: State Company, 1910.

Hassler, William W., *A. P. Hill: Lee's Forgotten General*. Richmond: Garrett and Massie, 1957.

Henry, Robert S., *Story of the Confederacy*. Indianapolis: Bobbs-Merrill Company, 1931, 1936.

Humphreys, Andrew A., *The Virginia Campaign of '64 and '65*. New York: Charles Scribner's Sons, 1883.

Johnson, R. U., and Buel, C. C., *Battles and Leaders of the Civil War*. New York: Century Company, 1887–1888.

Lee, Susan P., *Memoirs of William Nelson Pendleton, D.D.* Philadephia: J. B. Lippincott Co., 1893.

Long, Armistead L., *Memoirs of Robert E. Lee*. New York: J. M. Stoddart and Co., 1886.

Longstreet, James, *From Manassas to Appomattox*. Philadelphia: J. B. Lippincott Co., 1896.

McCabe, William G., *Memories and Memorials*, ed. by Armistead C. Gordon. Richmond: Old Dominion Press, 1925.

Marshall, Charles, *An Aide-de-Camp of Lee*, edited by Sir Frederick Barton Maurice. Boston: Little, Brown and Co., 1927.

Mercer, Philip, *The Gallant Pelham*. Macon, Ga.: J. W. Burke Company, 1929.

Smith, Daniel E. Huger, Smith, Alice R. Huger, and Childs, Arney H., editors, *The Mason Smith Family Letters, 1860–1868*. Columbia: University of South Carolina Press, 1950.

Snowden, Yates, and Cutler, H. G., *History of South Carolina*. New York: Lewis Publishing Company, 1920.

Sorrel, G. Moxley, *Recollections of a Confederate Staff Officer*. New York: Neale Publishing Co., 1905.

Southern Historical Society Papers. Richmond: 1876–.

Taylor, Walter H., *General Lee: His Campaigns in Virginia 1861–1865*. Norfolk, Virginia: Nusbaum Book and News Company, 1906.

Tucker, Glenn, *High Tide at Gettysburg*. Indianapolis: Bobbs-Merrill Co., 1958.

United States, Naval War Records Office, *Official Records of the Union and Confederate Navies in the War of the Rebellion*. Washington: Government Printing Office, 1894–1922.

United States War Department, *List of Field Officers, Regiments, and Battalions in the Confederate States Army, 1861–1865*. Washington: Government Printing Office, n.d. (189–?).

United States War Department, *List of Staff Officers of the Confederate States Army, 1861–1865*. Washington: Government Printing Office, 1891.

United States War Department, *The War of the Rebellion: A Compilation of the Official Records of the Union and Confederate Armies*. Washington: Government Printing Office, 1880–1901.

Wellman, Manly Wade, *Giant in Gray*. New York: Charles Scribner's Sons, 1949.

Wells, Edward L., *Hampton and His Cavalry in '64*. Richmond: B. F. Johnson Publishing Company, 1899.

Wise, Jennings C., *The Long Arm of Lee*. Lynchburg: J. P. Bell Company, 1915.

Wright, Marcus J., *General Officers of the Confederate Army*. New York: Neale Publishing Company, 1911.

Index

173